MW00736739

Presented To:

_____

From:

_____

Date:

_____

DESTINY IMAGE BOOKS BY JACK AND TRISHA FROST

Experiencing Father's Embrace
Spiritual Slavery to Spiritual Sonship

UNBOUND

Breaking Free from Life's Entanglements

JACK & TRISHA FROST

DESTINY IMAGE® PUBLISHERS, INC.
P.O. Box 310, Shippensburg, PA 17257-0310
"Promoting Inspired Lives."

This book and all other Destiny Image, Revival Press, MercyPlace, Fresh Bread, Destiny Image Fiction, and Treasure House books are available at Christian bookstores and distributors worldwide.

For a U.S. bookstore nearest you, call 1-800-722-6774.
For more information on foreign distributors, call 717-532-3040.
Reach us on the Internet: www.destinyimage.com.

ISBN 13 TP: 978-0-7684-4131-4
ISBN 13 Ebook: 978-0-7684-8830-2

For Worldwide Distribution, Printed in the U.S.A.
4 5 6 7 8 / 16 15 14 13

Dedication

I dedicate this book to my children and their spouses: Micah and Majesta Frost, Doug and Sarah Crew, and Joshua and Holly Frost. You have been there to walk me through the most difficult days of my life. You have given me the wisdom and counsel that makes me proud to be your mom. You have spoken truth to me when I needed truth spoken, and yet helped me understand my weaknesses while not focusing on them. You believed in me, the person I am, more than stumbling over what some people in the world think I should be. You have instead helped me make the choices that moved me forward in my strengths. You have made plans for my prosperity and lived to give and not take from me. How awesome is that?!

Special Acknowledgments

To my brother Cape and his wife Brenda: you were there then and now. I could always cry with you guys when I hurt and you made sure I was never left alone…this is family being family.

I also want to thank Johnnie and Kay Lewis, Bob and Kelly Parr, and all of our friends—you know who you are. To my team and executive board members: Dave and Kris Toyne, and Chip Judd, who never forgot that I was still their friend even without Jack beside me. You have all helped me walk out the transition of all that life brings, especially when it is not what you were expecting. You have helped keep me focused on the rest of my destiny.

To Bill and Beni Johnson: for the encouragement and the challenge that you brought to me after the loss of Jack. Your wisdom, prayer, and love for me and my family, when we were just a little more than strangers to you personally, were a true example of the Church being the Church. Your book *Strengthen Yourself in the Lord* is literally the reason that I am able to write this book.

To John and Carol Arnott: you also believed in me. I am forever grateful to you and the courage it took to host a revival that revived my family. Thank you for your forever friendship.

To John and Paula Sandford: for exampling what it is to be a true pioneer. Your wisdom has helped to form the character that Jack and I were able to live out with our family, and then in turn were able to give to the world.

To Paul and Sue Manwaring: for all the love and support that you shared even during the times when we had no clue. You promoted us behind the scenes without ever considering yourselves or desiring any recognition from us.

And finally to my pastors, Howie and Terri Russell, and Marc and Lisa Tueni: for the honor you have shown me and for creating a culture in our church that believes everyone is important and everything they have to say is important. You have valued me personally more than the gift within me and have always helped me to look at my destiny and stay on track with my identity. Thank you.

I am a fairly young widow when you consider the life span of most people in my generation. So what will the rest of my life look like? I'm not sure, but one thing I know is that with the wonderful support I have surrounding me, it won't be nearly as difficult as it could have been.

Thanks to all of you who loved me to life during the greatest transition and crisis I have ever lived through.

With deep appreciation,
Trisha Frost

Endorsements

Unbound is a book that is full of life. Life in the good times and life in the bad. Trisha shared beautifully her and Jack's stories on their life. How making decisions can affect your future and your family as well. The tools that Trisha shares in *Unbound* are most valuable to find help and healing. I found *Unbound* to be enlightening, and I highly recommend this great book. Thank you Trisha for once again being so transparent.

Beni Johnson
Bethel Church, Redding, California
Author of *The Happy Intercessor*

On March 5, 2007, the world became much poorer, but Heaven became much richer, as Jack Frost was promoted to Heaven.

My journey after receiving the baptism of love was upgraded as Jack and Trisha Frost invited me to spend a week together in Conway, South Carolina. Through their impartation, my life, family, relationships, and ministry were totally transformed.

You're about to discover joy, freedom, healing, and love as Trisha gives you the language of Heaven that will also upgrade your identity, and be released to dream to a higher level with Father God. Trisha is a dream releaser who gives eagle Christians an opportunity to soar higher and farther.

The spiritual climate in your life will be transformed. Get ready!

Leif Hetland
President, Global Mission Awareness
Author of *Seeing Through Heaven's Eyes*

Trisha Frost's book, *Unbound,* has the ability to take the reader to a place to not only recognize their hurt, but give them the tools to be made whole and move forward. As Trisha becomes vulnerable and opens up about her own life, it gives the reader a powerful example of how to overcome in sometimes the most difficult of circumstances. I recommend this book to hurt people looking to finally get past that which has kept them from moving on and to inspire that overcoming is possible in any circumstance.

Randy Clark
Global Awakening

This book "moved" me as I remembered Jack Frost and his revelation of the Father's love, which he brought to the Body of Christ. What a joy to see his wife Trisha now championing this same message, to penetrate our orphanness, and to heal the crippling inner fears of the heart.

John and Carol Arnott
Catch the Fire, Toronto
Author of *The Father's Blessing* and *Forgiveness*

I had the wonderful pleasure of knowing the late Jack Frost, whose message about the heavenly Father's love changed my life. Today, his message continues through his wife Trisha, who is a skilled Bible teacher and gifted minister. In this special book, Trisha blends her life experiences and biblical insights with teachings from her husband to create a masterful book about spiritual freedom in Christ. Whether you are dealing with grief, emotional pain, fear, or other paralyzing emotions, this book will help you find the grace needed for full recovery.

J. Lee Grady
Author and speaker
Director, The Mordecai Project
Former Editor of *Charisma Magazine*

David's dependence on the Lord is reflected in Psalm 25 where he learned to *"fix your eyes on the Lord and He will pull your feet out of the net."* Entangled by the net around Trisha's feet, the miracle of Father's love set her free from this entanglement of strongholds resulting from lie-based beliefs. Breaking free from the restrictions of environmental, social, marital, emotional, and spiritual woundedness, this breakthrough set Trisha's sails on an exciting, Holy Spirit, wind-driven adventure of victorious prayer and Father-love miracles, keeping the legacy of Jack and the ministry of Shiloh Place alive! This book is a truly great encouragement to help people break free of life's entanglements! A must to read as you embrace Father's unconditional love and His undaunted attention to your total well-being!

Dr. Howie and Terri Russell
Senior Leaders of The Father's House
Author of *The Wind Driven Church*

This book will change you! After reading chapter one, you will not be able to put the book down. Each story in each chapter draws you into an emotional experience where you are given the opportunity to change, to find freedom, to become whom we were meant to be. Another classic from the Frosts!

Steve Long
Senior Pastor of Catch The Fire Toronto
(Formerly TACF)

This book is a beautiful expression of God's healing love in the midst of loss, grief, and pain. Trisha artfully weaves her stories with Jack's last writings to create a complete picture of a Father who loves His kids and provides a safe refuge in the storms of life.

We were honored and privileged to be counted as Jack's friends, and we're equally honored to call Trisha our friend.

Thank you Trisha for having the courage, tenacity, and most of all the love to carry this message. You have taught us well to hold tightly to the hand of our loving Father through all the seasons in life.

Dave and Kris Toyne
Senior Leaders of Agape Christian Family Church
Clear Lake, Iowa

Trisha Frost carries on the legacy of the Father's love embodied in her husband Jack's life and ministry. *Unbound* is overflowing with heartfelt testimonies, helpful teaching, and the healing touch of a loving God.

Ed Piorek
Father Loves You Ministries

This book is a deep testimony. Deep in every respect. Trisha's experience of life, the power released from her own overcoming, and the resulting teaching and revelation. It prophesies another chapter of freedom for everyone of us brave enough not just to read it but apply it to our lives. This is a real book, learned out of the reality of a very real life, but presented in such a way that we can all access the fruit of her life and apply it to our own. Yet again the Frosts help this move of God to gain more momentum as the sons and daughters are set free and revival can be passed from one generation to the next. Read, enjoy, digest, and be forever changed into the free sons and daughters of our glorious King.

Paul Manwaring
Director of Global Legacy, Bethel Church
Author of *What on Earth is Glory?*

Why, since you wounded this heart, don't you heal it? (St. John of the Cross). Jack and Trisha, our hearts are grateful for the words you have written, words that will help many to find healing for the wounded heart! Reading *Unbound* left me breathless. You have presented to the Body of Christ a book that is so profound and yet so practical. What makes it so profound is that it is written by two people that know the pain of a wounded heart. What makes it so practical is that you have discovered the answers for those that have been wounded by the sting of shame and the gash of guilt. You have shown us how to be free from fear and how to once again enjoy the embrace of Father's love. Thank you!

Don Milam
Author of *The Ancient Language of Eden*

When Lazarus walked out of his own tomb, he was alive but he was still bound. Jesus told those around Lazarus to remove the grave clothes that restricted him from walking freely. In her exceptional book, *Unbound*, Trisha Frost - alongside her husband Jack, now unbound in glory - gives us indispensable wisdom on how to 'unbind' those who have come alive in Christ. Far too many Christians today are forgiven but not free, saved but still sick. Far too many ministries focus on getting people born again but not on getting people healed and discipled in Abba Father's love. Trisha's book will help to rectify that trend and realign the church's priorities. Indeed, I believe that for decades to come, *Unbound* will be a classic manual of freedom and a standard textbook on healing life's hurts. This is a book that none of us can afford not to buy and apply.

Dr Mark Stibbe
Founder and Leader of the Father's House Trust
Author of *I Am Your Father*, *Every Day with the Father*, *The Father You've Been Waiting For* and *From Orphans to Heirs*.

Being a leader is a difficult thing. It requires that people follow. Many times people do not follow very well. What complicates being a leader even more is when you follow a legend like Jack Frost. Trisha Frost, with the writing of this book, has succeeded in following a legend very well. Reader, prepare to be *Unbound*.

Cape and Brenda Grice, Majors
The Salvation Army

Contents

Foreword

I'll never forget the first time I met Jack Frost. He brought his son to attend our school of ministry here in Redding, California. I had heard of him, but this was the first time we had a chance to meet. We shared a meal together, after which he entrusted to us his treasure—his wonderful son Joshua.

His visit to Redding was a surprise for me. After realizing that we had this gifted man visiting our city, we asked him to speak to the church at our Friday night service. He graciously said yes. I was not prepared for what happened next. His message to the church was amazing. I sat there stunned. I also made mental notes during his message that I must take time to listen to it again. It was too insightful and weighty to listen to only once. I've heard many things through the years worth remembering, but none more so than what I heard that night. I was astounded by Jack's grasp of the heavenly Father's nature and heart for people. His ability to speak with healing wisdom to the broken condition of humanity impressed me deeply. That message became a reference point for thought, identity, and life itself. The impact of that one night still resonates within my heart.

Unbound: Breaking Free of Life's Entanglements is a continuation of that night—profound and empowering. It's an unusual book in that both Jack and his wife wrote it. Trisha took Jack's unpublished writings and put them together with her own to make a book that is full of wisdom with practical insights. It gives us an unusual glimpse of the profound revelation of God they carried as a team. This book truly fulfills the expectation given in its title—it is a manual to freedom. Captain Jack, as he was affectionately called, was a great storyteller. His experiences at sea are sobering, yet used with brilliance. He brings his unforgettable life experiences to us in a way that gives memorable insights for daily life. Jesus often taught that way. He taught us eternal truths in neatly packaged, unforgettable life experiences in a way that was hard to forget. Jack does the same. And now Trisha operates in that same gift.

People who first served in jobs outside of vocational ministry tend to become much more practical in their ministry. In other words, what they bring to the table must be doable. Being forced to learn Kingdom principles outside of the four walls of the church is a perfect training ground. It has proven to be the perfect school once again, as both Jack and Trisha bring us truth refined by the fire of human experience. Thankfully, they take us beyond theory into Kingdom reality.

In 2007 Jack went home to be with the Lord. But the message continues strong. His family, the first to benefit from Jack's personal journey from dysfunction to becoming an amazing husband and father, has picked up the mantle beautifully. Through them the message and the ministry continue. If you think about it, the greatest testament to the authentic nature of any message and the man who lived it is the effect it had on those who knew him best: his wife and children. They have given themselves to release this truth to places that Jack didn't have time to go.

Trisha states, "Healing takes your greatest shame and then anoints you to minister to others in the very areas you have hurt." She courageously models this truth in a way that makes you realize that the message of the Father's heart has just started to be proclaimed.

Bill Johnson
Bethel Church
Redding, California
Author of *When Heaven Invades Earth*
and *The Essential Guide to Healing*

Introduction

Men are anxious to improve their circumstances, but are unwilling to improve themselves; they therefore remain bound.—James Allen[1]

If I have learned anything in life, it is that seasons of life come and go. Change happens, and whether or not you embrace it will determine if you have a successful outcome or not. One of the most important things to Jack and me in our journey on this Earth is to leave a legacy so that our children have a platform to begin their lives on. A part of our journey has included letting go of things we cannot control, or should not control, so we can embrace the change needed for successful living. Choosing this stance in our daily living has, on many occasions, helped us to live "unbound" and free of life's entanglements to things that could cause a negative outcome in our life. Life itself does not always turn out the way we think it should. It is in those moments that we all learn what we are full of.

We also have learned there is nothing outside of eternity on this Earth that will last forever, except the love of Father God.

Life brings with it many choices to embrace courage and live our destiny. When living by His plan, life can be and is truly good. At times the letting go means letting go of something or someone very dear and precious to you in order to move forward into your destiny.

W.E.B. Du Bois once said, "One of the most important things to remember is this: To be ready at any moment to give up what you are, for what you might become."[2]

This lesson has helped me in being able to write this book. It is why the chapters of this book are named the way they are. Let go (break free) and embrace change that liberates you into a life that is not bound by circumstance or situation.

In order to fully present to the reader the idea that life can and should be a joyful and successful event, it is necessary to address the woundedness in our lives.

I know there is a danger in talking about woundedness. It might cause a person to focus more on their pain than upon God's ability to bring about life in their destiny. This can create a *victim mentality*, a belief that others are responsible for our pain. In understanding the negative influences of our past relationships, we must be willing to take personal responsibility for our choices to love or to hate. The degree of wholeness that we walk in is best determined by the degree of love that we demonstrate in our daily lives. The degree of true love that flows forth from us can best be measured by our ability to forgive those who have unjustly wounded us. The harder we find it to forgive, the smaller the measure of true love that is revealed. Relationships, at times, with those who are the hardest to love can become the very soil from which humility is birthed. As we humble ourselves to take responsibility for our part in the wounding, we are then exalted into the Father's presence.

Through the sharing of our own personal pain, we hope to accomplish being able to help others focus on cause and effect rather than fault and blame.

My desire for you is that you will understand that you are not responsible for the wounding that has occurred in your life through others, but you are responsible for your negative reactions to the wounding. I desire that you will be granted wisdom that brings about hope and encouragement to uproot and tear down, to destroy and overthrow the strongholds of your life, so you can truly build and *plant strongholds of love* that will cause you to have *no regrets* when your history is recorded.

Have I not commanded you? Be strong and of good courage; be not afraid... (Joshua 1:9).

As I have made daily choices to let go of fear and embrace courage, my life has continued to be fulfilling.

So the story begins....

Endnotes

1. James Allen, *As a Man Thinketh,* (New York: Cosimo Classics, 2010), 18. This book was originally published in 1918.

2. This quote was accessed off of http://www.wisdom quotes.com/quote/w-e-b-du-bois.html on January 21, 2012.

Chapter 1

Breaking Free of Loss and Embracing Trust

(Trisha)

"In Jesus' name we speak life, Jack, we need you! Life and healing, Jack!" These were the words being spoken into the phone by two of the greatest world leaders of our time, as Jack Frost, one of the greatest men of this era laid in a coma awaiting a great miracle or awaiting going home. As I gently laid the phone back next to Jack's ear, I felt a shift in the atmosphere around me as we all waited with great expectation for a great miracle to take place. People filled our brand new home on the waterway just wanting to be a part of this great event; this great miracle that we all felt now was just a matter of minutes away.

Friends, family members, and worship leaders came from all around the world to participate in our miracle and to stand by this great man's side as they poured their love and gratitude into him for all he had done to help them break free of their own personal hells.

After all, months had been spent in daily prayer for our miracle. So as we, Jack's family and friends, positioned ourselves for this miracle, the anticipation of his healing caused the atmosphere in the Frost home to be electrifying. But no one in the room anticipated what was about to happen next.

"Did you see it, did you see it?" came the words of the person standing beside Jack's bed.

"See what?" I responded.

"The angel; the angel that just came into the room." Perplexed, with no one knowing what to say or how to respond, the room filled with silence. You could have heard a pin drop as all eyes focused on me and the person who had seen the angel. Everyone in the room were born-again Christians, but I was not as sure about the guy who had seen this angel.

The angel's arrival was what we had all been waiting for—a miracle, a messenger with power that would have gotten Jack up out of his dreary hospital bed centered in the middle of our living room. The bed had literally become a prison for him, his own personal tomb. The boats traveling up and down the waterway were his only source of entertainment as he lay there day after day. He had been trapped in this prison for weeks, barely able to move.

With the news of the angel's entrance into the room, I was able to gather all of my strength to hope again. Could this be the moment? Were we about to experience what we had prayed and hoped for, for over 13 months? Anticipation was the emotion as all eyes waited for the next few seconds to unfold.

Once Jack slipped into the coma, I, Jack's wife and caregiver, had lost all hope that he would be healed. I had no strength left for this battle. Weary and emotionally drained from the daily barrage of the *why* questions, I had to release Jack to *break free* of his sickly prison and go home to his reward. So I bent down beside him and gently whispered into his ear, "Jack, I will be alright if you need to go home. I release you."

There is only so much a person in their humanness can experience as you watch the most changed individual, your soul mate and a person loved by the whole world, lay day after day in agonizing pain. It is especially hard after you have prayed with thousands of people for healing. Needless to say, I can only imagine what the torment was like for Jack, the person who was experiencing the pain of cancer running rampant through his body and totally destroying this normally very healthy individual.

Now the moment we anticipated had arrived. The angel was here! Had I given up too soon? I wondered as we watched to see what would happen next. To our chagrin, it was the angel of death. Our patriarch was going home. Strange as it might sound, as all eyes began to gaze upon Jack, the angel arrived and his facial expression changed from that of someone in intense pain to one of the biggest smiles I had ever seen. At first only his very close friend, Bob, had noticed it; but we knew once our attention was drawn to it. This formally hard, intense, and emotionally detached fishing boat captain, "Captain Blithe off the HMS Bounty," as nicknamed by his old crew and family members who knew him well; this hard-nosed, type A personality turned lover, mentor, and father to many had just come *face to face* with the loving Father whom he had given his life, right down to his final breath, to help others experience.

Just days before, Chip, one of his best friends, asked him, "Jack, how can I help you?" The response was to just keep doing what Jack no longer could. This type of spoken blessing motivated Chip to make sure he did exactly what his friend knew him capable of.

In the early hours of that Monday morning, Jack Frost had truly experienced all that he had spent years longing for. I could not help but smile to myself as I watched him lay there experiencing the *embrace of his Father. He had gone home.*

So many of us fear death. We fear the realization that we will have to relate healthily at some point in an eternal relationship with a Father. For those of us still left with a *love deficit* in our lives, this could possibly be a very scary event. We are loved throughout our lives but there are times that love may not have been expressed to us in a way that met our need, thus leaving a wound in our emotions that can cause pain for us and others. Our image of Father God may be determined by wounding that occurs in our formative years from our parents. This wounding is normally the beginning or source of most relationship problems.

Even though it was 3 A.M., the house was still filled with people. These people were like sheep without a shepherd. They did not know what to do or where to go now. We had all expected a miracle and were planning a revival service as soon as Jack got up. People did not know how to respond as they waited to be led. I guess it was how the disciples might have felt when they asked Jesus, "Where else will we go or what else will we do?" (See John 6:68). I could feel the eyes penetrating my soul. Glances from around the room now focused on my response. Would I respond with disappointment, grief, or sorrow? Or would I freak out?

I barely remember hearing the words of the funeral home director that night as he gave us the news that Jack was really gone. I felt like I was in a daze as I was instantly taken back in time to another day, another death of another great man in my life, my earthly dad.

It was a sunny day in June 1975 in Marion, South Carolina. Just a perfect day to visit the local ice cream shop for a double scooped cone of Bill's favorite lemon ice cream. Bill and Evie Grice were celebrating great news that he had been given a clean bill of health. Less than 24 hours later this man dropped dead while lighting up his very last cigarette. For years he had experienced problems with his heart. Being an adventurous person, Bill had lived his dream. He was a long distance truck driver and often drove through the night. In order to stay awake he would take bennies, a type of pill that causes your heart to beat faster, keeping him awake all night so he could haul his load faster than any other trucker.

The Grice family knew what it was like to not have their dad with them most of the time. They became used to being "fatherless" during the week so that they could have their dad on the weekends. None of us knew the damage that was occurring inside of his body. It wasn't until years later, after a heart attack while driving his eighteen-wheeler, did we find out.

This man, though not as well known to the world as my husband, loved me unconditionally and taught me many life lessons. He was my source of love. He was a girl's kind of dad. I could count on him for everything, including the emotional things a girl needed, or so I thought.

I remembered the pain of this night as the devastating news came—my hero of men was gone. I remembered the pain of judgment coming from my heart *that God is unfaithful when it comes to healing*.

In the next moment, like a dream within a dream, I was instantly taken back to a day in time when a little 6-year-old girl fought for sleep in the back of the family station wagon. Immediately after my dad had his first heart attack, my older brother piled me and another brother into the back of this car, with my dad in the front seat, and sped to the hospital in an effort to save this man's life. No one was allowed to talk or make any noise that might cause tension until we arrived at the emergency room entrance. Once there, the nurses would run out with a gurney, take my dad, and rush him inside. My other brother and I were left alone in the car with no one to comfort us or explain to us all that was happening.

Weeping uncontrollably, I cried out to the only source I knew that could help us. I prayed to my heavenly Father to please help my daddy to live. My mom was a pretty helpless person, sickly most of her life, so my older brother was left to carry the responsibility for us as kids. I knew he was too young to have to leave school and provide for us should my dad not make it. Knowing the responsibility my brother shouldered caused me to pray even harder for my dad.

We lived expecting that at any moment our dad may no longer be around. It was years before that dreadful day came. My dad finally experienced a heart attack that basically caused his heart to explode inside of his body. I was a teenager by this time and had long ago decided that God was good. I thought serving Him was better than going to hell, but believed His power to be limited. I made many harsh judgments toward God while growing up in an environment where I was taught to serve God in order to be loved, and as long as I obey Him, I would make it into Heaven. It seemed to me an ordinary way to think. I often felt exasperated when it seemed my prayers went unanswered. I prayed for healing and finances so that our basic needs would be met.

I thought that if God is not powerful enough to heal and provide then I will go to work and take care of myself. (This was a lie, an ungodly belief, that my heart embraced as truth and thus became my reality.) *I was capable of doing a better job than He was* seemed a natural response in my mind and it became the way I lived my life after my dad died.

It never dawned on me that I was developing a way of thinking that would alienate me from God for years to come. I believed and therefore became a very independent person. This particular way of thinking is called a *stronghold.*

Strongholds are developed from our habits (an act repeated so often that it becomes involuntary, there is no new decision of mind each time the act is performed). Strongholds can also be birthed from judgments that have been made when wounding occurs or when the basic needs of life are not met.

Every human being has built inside of them basic needs. We all have a need to *feel unconditional love.* Even if we did not act right or perform right, there is this need to be able to feel that we are loved. When we know we are loved and valued by another, we then develop a sense of security.

In this place of *security*, our value is expressed through a sense of belonging. Once we feel we are valued by another and are secure in their presence, we will become more secure with people in our lives. This sets us up to be able to embrace their blessings and wisdom, thus having an atmosphere created for us to believe in praise, affirmation, and value.

We were created to live in an atmosphere of *praise, affirmation, and value.* In this type of environment we become aware of our purpose in life.

This is the place where we sense a *purpose* from God and make decisions to live our destiny.

When these needs are not being met, a wound cuts into the soul of a person. Sometimes, if wounds are not dealt with, *mental strongholds* are developed. Under the negative influence of a stronghold, a breeding ground, a source of all sorts of demonic activity, can begin to live.

Strongholds of negative thinking can actually develop a belief structure that for the wounded person becomes their truth and develops into their life's reality.

Joseph Goebbels, Hitler's Master of Propaganda, convinced Hitler that if you tell people a lie long enough they will begin to believe it. Hitler used this tactic in convincing his leaders that the Jewish culture needed to be annihilated, thus carrying out the greatest mass murder of our time.

Many times patterns of thinking become a way of living that will develop in a person's life without them even realizing it. Negative thinking that causes a person to develop negative habit patterns often results in the wounding of those we love. It causes some of the greatest relational problems we face today in our society. Wounding can happen without any true understanding as to why we would intentionally or unintentionally hurt someone, but habit patterns have a life of their own.

Bishop Charles Green reported that 58 percent of Americans have mild to moderate mental health problems, 24 percent have moderate to major mental health problems, 82 percent are relationally and emotionally unhealthy, and 80 percent of all marriages are in trouble.

Some of the signs of emotionally unhealthy traits are:

- Selfishness
- Pleasure-seeking mentality
- Living in a dream or fantasy world
- Irresponsibility
- Disregard of consequences of behavior
- Lack of self-discipline
- Depression
- Phobias
- Addictions
- Anxieties
- Dysfunctional behavior—don't trust, don't talk, and don't feel.

Often these habit patterns of thinking turn into mental strongholds within our minds. Usually, they are developed in our family of origin because of woundedness and love deficits we have experienced in that environment.

Now, not only was my dad not there to provide for my emotional needs, but my husband was also gone. I have had much ministry over the loss of my dad and the feeling of being abandoned by him as well as by Father God; so why did I immediately slip back into those old thought patterns as soon as Jack was given his death sentence?

Habit patterns of thinking, or strongholds, can be hidden so deep within the subconscious that you are literally not aware of them until you get bumped in your emotions. I had been bumped!

My judgment or ungodly belief had become, *You can only count on the men in your life to provide just enough to get by, and then they will abandon you. So if you want to be provided for, then go out and make it happen for yourself.*

Living this lie, which became truth for me—my truth and thus my life's reality—kept me from being able to trust the most important men in my life for years to come: my dad, my husband, my brother, my pastor, and my mentors that came in and out of my life over the years. It seemed to me a steady stream of people in my life that I would never be able to completely trust. If I did let my guard down, I would be disappointed and eventually abandoned.

My inability to trust wounded those around me who tried to help me live my life successfully. My stronghold of thinking became, *I will only allow certain people into certain areas of my life.* Those who tried to get close to me could feel this invisible wall, this fortress of lack of trust, and they could only lead me so far before they hit my wall.

Strongholds are characterized by habit patterns of thought that exist in the area of our soul, mind, will, emotions, and personality. They are hidden so deeply within our soul that they have the ability to influence the negative thought patterns of our life.

Strongholds are habitual lies that we have embraced at the core of our inner being. They are built by a foundation of lies and half-truths. They have become a fortress of thought that influences the way we respond to the truth about God's character within us.

Strongholds are spiritual fortresses of thought where demonic influences may hide and be protected. Any area of darkness within our thoughts is an open door to demonic activity. Satan traffics in darkness. Father God traffics in light.

Strongholds exalt themselves above the knowledge of God and give negative forces a secure place to influence our mind, will, and emotions (see 2 Cor. 10:4).

Strongholds are wrong motivations and attitudes that protect and defend a person's walk in the flesh.

Strongholds can lie so deeply within our soul that we don't recognize them as sin, but instead take on the attitude, "That is the way I have always been. This is the way my family is. It is my cultural or ethnic background. How can I expect to be any different?"

Strongholds can keep a person from repentance. Lack of repentance hinders the healing process, thus the habitual fortress of thought is not broken within them.

Strongholds have a sick core. Much like an infection that needs to be lanced so that the poison can drain and the infected area healed, if the stronghold is not dealt with, twisted thoughts and emotions spread poison throughout the soul.

There is a *purpose behind mental strongholds.* They are there to alienate us from believing we are loved by Father God. Mental strongholds do this in many ways:

- They produce negative thoughts within us in order to block us from giving or receiving love.

- They restrict our knowledge of God.

- They can give us tunnel vision so we can't see wrong from right.

- They shape our value system and how we value others.

- They distort our priorities in life.

- They hinder us from walking in the truth.

- They can make straight thinking difficult by guarding our weak spots with false feelings and emotions.

- They send negative messages to our soul.

- They cause us to draw negative conclusions regarding how we relate to people.

- They cause us to do things we don't want to do.

When our thoughts continue to dwell upon feelings of fear, insecurity, unbelief, doubt, lust, control, striving, unrest, bitterness, resentment, criticisms, unforgiveness, or habitual sin, a strong deceiving hold begins to build in us like a fortress. These responses of our flesh then automatically come forth from the habit structures of thought built within us.

Now as Jack, my hero, had gone home to be with his Father for all eternity—what would I choose to do? Would I allow my heart to be established? *"His heart is steadfast, trusting in the Lord. His heart is established; He will not be afraid..."* (Ps. 112:7-8). Or would I return to old habit patterns of thinking from the pain of my past?

It is in our identifying what makes us tick that these behaviors or habit patterns are uncovered so they can be dealt with. I often pray Psalm 139:23-24: *"Search me, O God, and know my heart; try me, and know my anxieties; and see if there is any **wicked** way in me, and lead me in the way everlasting."*

Would I allow my mental strongholds to be what is established in my heart or would I take this opportunity to choose courage?

The choice was mine to make. Hmmmmm, I choose…?

QUESTIONS TO PONDER

1. What are four emotional needs that each person has?

2. Which one of these needs has not been met in your own life, thus causing wounding to occur?

3. Can you name a habit pattern of thinking, or a stronghold that has caused you to embrace a lie as a truth and thus become a reality in your life?

4. Who are the ones who have brought wounding into your life and have contributed to your choices of not being able to trust?

5. Can you forgive those who wounded you?

SAMPLE PRAYER

Father, I want to trust those whom You have placed into my life to love me and mentor me and to be a part of providing my basic needs. I have judged You and (name people who you feel have been a source of wounding in your life) for not being there to provide these needs. I own my behavior and ask You to forgive me first for not taking the time to find Your plan for my life and for not trusting You.

I have been wounded and ask You to forgive me for believing lies that I have been abandoned and I have no value in Your heart or others' lives. I choose to forgive those who have wounded me (name them if you can). I trust in the blood of Jesus to sever all ungodly beliefs and place the cross between the lie and myself. I make a choice today to stop embracing the lies that my emotional needs will not be met. I choose to look first to You before man to meet those needs, and I believe You will surround me with those whom You have chosen to love me and speak into my life.

Father, help me to see who they are, and I ask for mercy to trust in Your wisdom.

Chapter 2

Sea of Fear: Breaking Free of the Fear That Entangles and Embarking on a New Life's Journey

(Jack)

"David, get in here before you are thrown overboard." The Captain continued to scream at David not to unsnap his lifeline but to get back into the safety of the warm wheelhouse. The freezing gale-force wind had abruptly come out of seemingly nowhere, and all of a sudden our calm, surreal night was about to turn into a nightmare.

We had been sailing very slowly and had decided to wind the canvas sails in for the night and go under motor power when the gale-force winds began to blow. "All hands on deck," the Captain shouted! "Snap your lifelines on and wind the sails in before the wind grabs the mast and flips the boat over into the cold waters of the Antarctic." Every man was given an assignment to get the boat secured. David, who had never been in open oceans before, yet was more of a seasoned sailor than the other seven inexperienced sailors, was given the most dangerous job of getting the sails on the bow secure.

Just moments before we had crossed the Strait from the tip of Antarctica. There was not even a breeze stirring on the ocean that night. It was our last night together as an expedition, so we all sat in the wheelhouse sharing our stories from the past three weeks of our journey to the Land of Ice. We shared all of the highs and lows of the greatest adventure that any human being could have left the warmth of home to be a part of.

All my life I have had a love affair with the ocean and my greatest dream in life was being fulfilled on this eight-man expedition to the continent of Antarctica.

Suddenly, gale-force winds came in from nowhere, which is very typical for this region of the Earth. They began to howl as we went from hearty laughs, as each of us listened intently to the exaggerated personal stories of our adventure, to screams of fear as the Captain began to holler and we, the greenhorn crew, went into action to save our very lives.

Again the Captain screamed out to David, hoping his voice would carry above the howls of the wind, but he still did not return to the wheelhouse, instead staying on the bow of the 70-foot Pelagic sailboat with a panic-stricken look on his face.

Maybe he was tripping and enjoying the ride of the gale-force winds that were taking the boat up in the air before the bottom would fall out as the water from the wave rolled under the boat. The boat was like a roller coaster ride. It was up and down like riding a mad bull.

These winds began to toss our boat around and take it in any direction they wanted it to go. Just seconds before there was such a calm on the ocean it almost seemed a little eerie. The eight-man crew was in the middle of Drake's Passage, known as the *Sea of Fear* to any seasoned sailor. We were underway with the tip of South America as our destination. Eight crazy, adventurous men and the crew of the expedition had decided to sail to Antarctica for a month of what we perceived to be the adventure of a lifetime.

The ride home had become somewhat boring until now and I realized that this perfect storm was what I, Captain Jack Frost, had come to this Ice continent for. The adventure! Ahhh!

But my friend David, a renowned artist from Massachusetts, had gotten his lifeline entangled in the ropes of the excessive bow sail and was in danger of losing his very life. Panic-stricken, the crew and captain tried to figure out how to rescue him but to no avail. He had broken the golden rule of sailing in rough seas. He unsnapped his lifeline. He had to unsnap the lifeline and reattach it while removing the entanglement of the ropes. Timing was crucial. If not timed exactly to the precise moment of the boat coming off the wave, David would be washed overboard with no way for us to retrieve his body. He literally would have been lost at sea.

Amongst the eight adventurers and three crewmembers were only two Christians, David and I. We were all so panic-stricken that no prayers were prayed to spare his life. In the middle of this Sea of Fear, panic was our only companion as we were paralyzed to help. There was nothing to trust in except a supernatural intervention.

Most people at some point find themselves in the same place David found himself; entangled in life's circumstances, not sure what the next moment in time is going to bring to them. Will you live or will you die? This depends largely on the choices we make to overcome fear or circumstances that hinder us in those relationships that bring life to us.

David was faced with a choice to just let go and end it all or to choose life. In choosing life he would have to overcome the greatest fear and obstacle he had ever faced. David told me later he kept hearing a voice saying "Live, Live, Live," and he knew that he had to choose to unsnap his lifeline, remove the entanglements, and reattach it in order to save his life. It would have been so much easier to give up than to muster the courage to be able to choose life.

David did choose to live and his life was spared that night as he watched one very large wave pick the bow of the boat completely out of the water and, as the boat dropped, unsnapped his lifeline, removed the entanglements, reattached his lifeline, and made it back to the warmth and safety of the wheelhouse.

Unable to speak, David pondered the choice he had made. He knew something was going to be forever different within him. He said he felt his hard heart, which he kept guarded even with his closest relationships, begin to soften. He could not articulate what had happened inside of him as he chose life that night, but he knew he would return home a different person; a person who longed to give away the love that had been given to him during the greatest crisis of his life. This was David's divine intervention.

It is in the Sea of Fear that we make our choices to break free of the entanglements of life that we find ourselves in bondage to. It is in the Sea of Fear *that our pain begins to outweigh our shame and we seek the change* that will lead us into the fulfillment of our purpose for life. It is in the Sea of Fear that we discover the hindrances that have almost drowned many of us. It is in the midst of the greatest fear of our life that we, like David, are faced with the decision to "Live, Live, Live."

We don't have to make a trip to Antarctica to figure out that most of us are entangled in our own life situations. But for me, David's experience caused me to want to identify what those things in my life were that kept me guarded from real intimacy with those who love me unconditionally. As I watched David over the next few months change from this hard, guarded personality to a soft and humble man, passionate about his family, I knew that the Father's love for us was not just an experience we had received during an encounter with Him, but rather this experience would become a road to healing for the world.

Knowing the Father in our crisis was the missing link for intimacy for me in all of my other relationships. Now I knew that I also had to make those same choices to live, not just physically, but in confronting my own personal fears that kept me on guard in all of my relationships. But how do we continue to get others to believe that if they choose to live, love will become their lifeline?

How do we show others the way to untangle their personal entanglements that prevent them from being a source of love, warmth, and safety to their families?

We first have to recognize that, for most of us, we live in that Sea of Fear.

- Fear of intimacy
- Fear of woundedness
- Fear of "what ifs"

- Fear of man
- Fear of what man thinks
- Fear of judgments
- Fear of failures
- Fear of being loved
- Fear of giving love

Admitting that we have fear is the first step toward healing.

I too went home from the greatest adventure of a lifetime to embrace the next great adventure of becoming this gift of love to my family first. Even though over the previous years I had had an encounter that changed my image of how I viewed love, my trip to Antarctica reminded me of a few more entanglements that helped me realize *that healing life's hurts is a process.* But the process has to have its beginnings.

The list of fears is an endless list that, if we continue to allow, will drown us. The effects of living in the Sea of Fear on our relationships keeps us from our purpose in life; our purpose in life to believe we are loved, so out of that belief, we are able to love others.

The majesty of Antarctica was a breathtaking experience. As my human spirit delighted in the magnificent beauty, and the age and uniqueness of each individual iceberg, I realized just how insignificant I have viewed myself to be.

Like those icebergs, I believe that in choosing life, my purpose in this world is so significant that others will feel my love and be motivated to live their dream and live out their destinies.

Deciding to leave the Sea of Fear and embrace the choice of taking a risk to allow myself to be loved so I may be able to love was the beginning of my healing process. This was not the end, but rather the beginning of a journey that would take me and our family into the greatest adventure life could offer. (Read *Experiencing Father's Embrace* by Jack Frost, which is available from Destiny Image.)

It will free us from a life where past addictions, hurts, wounds, and behaviors have caused us to stay in bondage to a loveless life.

QUESTIONS TO PONDER

1. What are some of the fears (entanglements) in your life that cause you to live hindered by life situations? (Name your Sea of Fear.)

2. If you fear intimacy in your life, can you remember a time or hurtful event that caused you to emotionally shut down?

3. What are some of the negative behaviors or fears that you might need to unsnap your lifeline from?

SAMPLE PRAYER

Father, I ask You to forgive me for choosing to allow fear to control my relationships. I have been hurt by (name the person or event), and the pain was so unbearable it caused me to fear being involved with people in my life. I ask You to forgive me for shutting my heart off to love, and thereby shutting my heart off to You. Your Word says perfect love casts off fear because fear is torment. I no longer want to be tormented by the fears in my life, and I ask You to forgive me for tormenting others through my pain.

I choose to unsnap my lifeline from all entanglements that hinder my relationships with You, my family, and those who I have been called to relate to. I receive Your perfect love, and through this love I cast away the torment of my soul, the fear that has caused me to embrace a lie that prevents me from totally trusting in Your love for me. In Jesus' name I choose to believe You and what Your plan is for my life. I ask You to renew the adventurous heart within me as I choose to live a life of courage.

Chapter 3

Breaking Free From the Cycle of Pain and Into the Cycle of Life

(Trisha)

TGIF! Friday, after work…Shirley was looking forward to her weekend for days now. It had been an exceptionally hard week at work. Being the assistant principal and P.E. instructor for a special needs elementary school was very rewarding but had many challenges during a day. These special needs children often exhibited very rough behaviors, and dealing with children who acted unruly and did not always understand why they were being disciplined could take its toll.

Shirley was a tall, athletic woman who could handle herself in almost any situation. She had been a coach for over 30 years now and it was just a normal part of her personality to be the one in charge. If there were no apparent leader, Shirley would become the leader as a matter of default. Her parents never trained her natural-born leadership skills properly and so they became a source of hindrance in her relationships in life.

Encouraged most of her life by her father to do it her way, this was the attitude she brought into her relationships with those she loved—her family. "If you can't help me, you are hurting me! So just move out of my way," was her belief. Her independent attitude was strength to her. She never saw that this could possibly wound the people around her and cause them to reject her. I used to tell her she would have made a great governor of her state, probably a great president, but growing up in the late 1920s and '30s, our country would have never received a woman as president. In her day, you could tell she had been a very beautiful woman, looking very much like the Swedish born actress of her era, Greta Garbo.

She moved to the Daytona Beach area in the late 1940s to accept a teaching position. Her attraction to dramatic flair landed her a place in a small drama and theatrical troop, where she met and married Barney Frost. A jock of a guy, she knew it would take a man's man to be able to handle her rough and tumble personality. Sure enough, after many years of fighting over who really wore the pants in this home and two children later, Barney had all he could handle of a woman who refused to at least listen to him and his input into their family. Barney was a businessman with his own small mechanic shop. He worked on race cars for the famous drivers who would come to the Daytona Beach Speedway with their fast cars.

He had been raised most of his life without a dad. Barney was called the town bastard, in the small town of Hephzibah, Georgia, because his dad abandoned them when he was just a young boy. None of the boys in the town were allowed to spend time with him and Barney was often ridiculed because of his father. He learned fast how to fight in order to defend his name.

Coming from the South, Barney was not reared to allow the woman to rule the home, no matter how capable she was of doing so. So after many years of living with a strong personality, Barney began to harden his heart toward her. Neither of them were aware of this slow process that led to the death of their 20-year relationship, but still it happened. Barney moved out of their bedroom after learning of a secret in her life that she evidently had hidden from him for many years. Her secret was of a previous marriage to another dysfunctional person. Not being able to confide in anyone was a stronghold of thought that Shirley had built into her thinking after living through the wounding of a past rejection, which ended in her being abandoned by her first husband.

Her strong-willed personality was just an attempt at self-preservation from being wounded again. When we enter into a relationship with woundedness, it creates *a cycle of pain* in our lives that subconsciously sets these negative thoughts into motion. As we think upon these negative thoughts, it becomes a stronghold in our mind, thus affecting our will and emotions.

Remember, if you believe a lie long enough it will become truth to you. As it becomes your reality, you are faced with life choices that can lead you into a lifestyle of sin and disobedience. Sin left unrepented creates a place of darkness in your life, in your mind, and, worst of all, finds its place into your heart, causing you to respond to your pain by either hurting others or refusing to allow others access to your heart.

This is just what our enemy—the devil—would like to see happen in all of our relationships. If he can keep you in that place of believing in the lie that comes with pain, then he has just gained access into an area of your heart.

Giving him a place in your life separates you from the very thing you have desired—someone to love and accept you. This in turn is an open door for demonic oppression in your life. Thus the cycle continues until somebody in some generation says no. No more.

The cycle of pain looks somewhat like the diagram on the following page.

CYCLE OF PAIN

Shirley had never told her family about this former life with another husband who also abandoned her. Not having family around her, she learned how to cope through the use of alcohol. It became her only source of comfort. It did not take long for it to become an addiction that she hid from most of the people in her life. She was the most amazing woman Monday through Friday, but come Saturday she became a "weekend warrior alcoholic."

"Jack Frost, you come out right now! Jack, I told you to come to me now!" In the distance you could hear the whimpers of a small, frightened little boy trying very hard not to be heard. He knew this tone from his mother's voice meant that she was in her "sickly mode," and if you happened to be caught at home you would become the object of her anger. For Shirley, anger was an emotion that she often expressed without a second thought. It had become for her how she dealt with her frustrations with Barney. Barney would leave Shirley at home by herself as he headed off to the bars to be around his tennis buddies. Feeling abandoned, she often turned that feeling into anger that was released on Jack. Jack scurried to make it to his hiding place underneath some old blankets at the very

WOUNDING
Prov 18:14 & 17:22

**DEMONIC
OPPRESSION**
Jude 6, Acts 26:18 &
Acts 10:38

**NEGATIVE
THINKING PATTERNS**
Prov 23:7a, Job 3:25 &
Hosea 2:5

DARKNESS
I John 1:5-7 & 2:10-11

**SIN AND
DISOBEDIENCE**
James 4:1 & 4:14-15

back of his bedroom closet. It was in this place of darkness and hiddenness that he escaped from his mother's abusive behavior. His older brother and dad had learned how to retreat to the tennis courts, but because of Jack's youth he was often left to fend for himself.

"I found you! Now I will teach you a lesson in how to obey!" Snatching Jack up and beating him severely was often the result of Shirley's torrents of unleashing her pent-up anger. Her cycle of pain was now becoming a generational habit structure of destruction that would cause Jack's own family, once he left his family of origin, much pain also.

Life happens and we make decisions from our own pain whether or not we are going to leave a cycle of pain for the next generation.

Life comes in cycles. First we are born—oh, the joy of the *goo goo gaa gaa* days. Next we enter the toddler era, the season of learning that distinct word, *no!*

Stage three is the drama king and queen, the preteen age of boys trying to figure out when they are going to develop and oh, the dread of premenstrual girls—no one truly does understand those wonderful adolescents.

Young adulthood offers us the phase of independence, either we begin our career choices or we leave and cleave to that person that "was made just for me and I could just eat them alive." (You just wait about five years and you will wish that you had eaten them.)

Real man- and womanhood is the next phase—my house, my rules. You find yourself married to that person you dreamed about in the last phase, but now you have children—the ultimate quest for manhood, to reproduce after our own kind. There have been moments in time that I am not so sure, while watching this person I help to create, that they are even human, much less my tribe or kind.

Then comes the golden years—the years that you dream about. Your responsibility to care for your children is over (or so you were told), they are on their own now. You have planned for retirement, and you and your wonderful spouse are going to live the dream of RVs and the cruise scene.

As you look back on your own personal cycle, if it looks anything like the one above, time flew by and what did you do to impact the world? When history is written about you, what will it say? I once read a saying, *"Whether you live good or bad, live to become a memory."* Now I am not sure I agree with this—who needs another bad memory?—but I understand the underlying principle to live so that your life is never forgotten. For me it has to mean something to others as well.

A scary thought is that someone would be remembered for the pain that they brought into the life of another individual, yet it happens every day. Remember Judas of Jesus' time? He lived to betray the greatest example of love that ever lived in human form. Is there any other memory of Judas?

There are so many people that, because of our proneness toward negative thoughts, remember only what they did rather than what their potential was and who they were created to be.

Many of us are not living out our greatest potential because we have absolutely no clue what it is. We have never known because no one has been there to speak life to us. John Lennon of the Beatles once said, "Life is what happens while you make other plans." [1]

Many of us have grown up in abusive homes, and this has caused us to be comfortable with abusive lifestyles. You think that this is just life or your lot in life. I don't think that the Creator of life ever intended for our lives *not* to be good.

But for some of us, just like that little boy Jack, the *"house of pain"* was the same home that we were forced to grow up in.

Here is a provoking thought: our parents were not the parents God intended for us to have. When Father God created us, He had a plan, a plan with hope for a future (see Jer. 29:11). Father God created each of us from His image of love (see 2 Cor. 3:18), but somewhere along the way that image became distorted and love was exchanged for pain. Pain leaves wounds and scars that sometimes just cannot be forgotten about. So this pain turns into a cycle of behavioral patterns that in turn causes us to become pain for those we love.

Jack lived in a very dysfunctional home with outwardly successful parents. I lived in a home where love abounded but my parents outwardly were not as successful.

I too had very dysfunctional behavioral cycles that have caused me to recycle this pain from my family of origin. This is the only time I can think of that it is not good to recycle.

When we look back at this cycle of pain that starts with the pain of a wound in our lives (you can name your own pain here), we see that most of our woundedness can be traced back to our love deficit. A person can only handle being wounded so many times before their ability to receive love is totally dried up inside of them and they are not able to give love to their own personal families, much less the world.

Wounding can cause us to start compacting our hurts, emotions, and feelings. Usually by the age of 35 or 40, the areas we have stuffed our pain into begin to leak out in our relationships and personality.

Some possible characteristics of wounding are:

1. Withdrawal or Isolation: We begin to cut ourselves off from people, thinking that others are not safe and they are the source of our pain. This is a form of controlling our relationships.

2. Walls of Self-Protection: Guarding ourselves from further hurt. Fear of man and past wounding can cause us to lose trust in our relationship with others.

3. Possessiveness: Bonding to only one or two people. Feeling threatened when others try to enter relationship with our one or two. At times, this leaves the one or two with feelings of being smothered. This can lead to emotionally dependent relationships.

4. Control and Manipulation: Deep inside we become insecure with other people. Because of past wounding, we have to be in control so our life will go better. If we can't control then we cut off intimacy to protect ourselves.

5. Difficulty in Receiving Correction or Instruction: We must trust a person to receive from them. When we have been wounded, we tend to harden our hearts and refuse to submit to any authority. We can become very opinionated and demand our own way.

6. Difficulty in Receiving or Giving Love and Acceptance: We must feel secure with a person in order to love them, but wounding has caused them to feel insecure with most people (so they cannot receive from them). Our heart may have become so hardened by the wounding, that we choose not to express our emotions or feelings.

7. Need for Constant Attention or Recognition: Most of us have a deep need for praise. If not given, then we might withdraw from the relationship.

8. Feel Unloved: When we are not valued in our relationships, we begin to feel betrayed. We can easily become suspicious of others. This can set us up for more rejection and blame shifting.

9. Self-Centeredness: Life and conversation focuses more on our needs, causing a "victim mentality."

10. Pattern or Broken Relationships: Fear of man causes us to become people pleasers—not saying what we feel but saying what others want to hear. Because of our distrust of others in the relationship, it hinders us from bonding in an emotional healthy way.

11. Find Identity in a Group: Finding our acceptance in belonging to this group can lead to becoming trapped in the group. The drug culture, homosexuality, or rebel groups are a few examples of this. You will go where you feel you fit. We fight hard to fit in because we have learned how to follow more than lead.

12. Judgmental Attitudes: Out of our wounding we begin to build ourselves up by putting others down. We surround ourselves with those who agree with us.

13. Lack Intimacy with God: We may blame God for the wounding that has come to our lives. Thus, our feeling toward authority is transferred to God. Our relationship with God then is based on our service because we are trying to be loved more. When we don't feel we have a close sense of His presence, then our efforts become our failures and we begin to feel shame that leads to guilt that causes us to hide from His advances.

14. Fears and Phobias: Wounding has led to the fear of man, rejections, and feelings of being a failure. You are only a failure when you blame others for your mistakes. Anxieties and panic attacks can begin here.

Being wounded can cause us to shut ourselves off to love. When we shut ourselves off to love, the stronghold of thought is built and exalts itself against the knowledge of God. God says that He is love (see 1 John 4:18) and that we have been made in the image of God (see 1 Cor. 3:18). But we choose to believe the lie that *nobody loves me, I am unloveable* when pain comes into our life. We might then choose to act on this pain and allow sin and disobedience into our lives. Giving to others what has been given to you is the personal anthem of many hurt people.

When we make a choice to deliberately hurt another person, it is considered a sin. Then we try and hide by denying that we did anything.

We tend to respond in one of three different roles:

1. Victim: As a victim we are incapable of dealing with wounding so we give into the pain. Wounding then leads to feelings of loneliness, to deep inner pain, to feelings of self-pity, to possible depression, to despair, to life without hope, and finally to thoughts of life being too painful to live (death wishes).

2. Persecutor: As a persecutor we will fight against the wounding through negative emotions and resentment, which leads to bitterness that in turn leads to hatred. Hatred then leads to rebellion against anyone, everyone, and everything, thus causing us to live a life as an abuser, rarely acknowledging a need to change.

3. Rescuer: Wounding creates a deep inner agony. The rescuer will struggle against the wound and become indifferent to the hurt. We will take on a superficial happiness and find recognition in being in the spotlight. We can become talkative, loud, and aggressive. We enjoy the praise of man through our own accomplishments of overcoming crisis. Through our experiences, others can also be helped out of their situations. Often we have no need for healing because we have overcome our pain through denial. We need to feel good about ourselves so we can help another deal with their wounds.

Not acknowledging our wounds can take us to a place of darkness in our lives. Once we live from that place of darkness, we are totally living from our flesh man. For me personally, I think all sin comes from a desire to live or protect my flesh. In any case, we run to a place of isolation or what I call darkness.

George MacDonald, in his book *Creation In Christ*, says that darkness is comprised of 12 thought patterns, followed by my explanation:

"I am my own king and my own subject." In other words, our lives revolve around ourselves.

"I am the center from which go out my thoughts." What can others do for me?

"I am the object and end of my thoughts." They begin with me and end with me.

"My own glory is, and ought to be, my chief care." What's in it for me? What draws attention to me?

"My ambition, to gather the regards of men to the one center, myself." This is drawing the praise and recognition of men to myself.

"*My* pleasure is *my* pleasure." I live for my own comfort and happiness. It doesn't matter how it disappoints or wounds another.

"My kingdom is—as many as I can bring to acknowledge my greatness over them."

"My judgment is the thoughtless rule of things." This is how I interpret them. Whatever I think is right is right and everyone else is wrong.

"My right is—what I desire." My rights are what I am in need of in order to enhance my position and greatness. What do I need to feel better about myself and draw others to me?

"The more I am all in all to myself, the greater I am." That is, I think that I'm greater as I'm wrapped up in myself.

"I am free with the freedom that consists in whatever I'm inclined to do, from whatever quarter may come the inclination." To do my own will is to be free and to live. This is the biblical standard of "not my will, Father, but Yours!"

"The less I acknowledge debt or obligation to another; the more self-sufficing I feel or I imagine myself—the greater I am."[2] I close my eyes to the fact that I did not make myself for myself. Thus, the more selfish and independent I become, the more freedom and greatness I feel. However, Second Corinthians 5:17 (as it relates to the spirit man) says, *Therefore, if anyone is in Christ, he is a new creation; old things have passed away; behold, all things have become new.*

When we live for ourselves, we love Father God not for who He is, but for what He can do for us. This is living life from a total selfish perspective. Living from the cycle of pain at our core keeps us trapped in our life's entanglements. We cannot just deal with one of the five issues in the cycle of pain, such as casting out a demon or dealing just with the woundedness of our past. But if we can begin a process that deals with the *root issues*, we can then get rid of the behavior and be set free in areas of our lives.

I believe that my greatest battle has never been with a demonic power, but instead has been with my flesh man. It has been my choices that I have made out of comforting my own flesh that have most often hindered me from growth and maturity. I want it my way, and my way now.

Satan is a defeated foe. The blood of Christ took care of this. So then why do we continue to see defeated people, defeated in their life circumstances and in relational issues? I think that yes, satan has a plan and his plan is to constantly bombard us with lies of deception, and that as we embrace them and apply them to our lives, we become like them. The way for us to continue to mature in the Lord is for us to bring truth (light) to those areas of our lives where deception is in control. We do this through renewing our minds with the concepts of God's love.

This cycle of pain can be broken once we are willing to identify and deal with the woundedness that has caused a love deficit in our lives. Becoming willing to deal with the issues so that we can focus on destiny is becoming willing to choose a lifestyle of courage.

QUESTIONS TO PONDER

1. Can you identify some of the wounded areas of your life that have left you dealing with pain?

2. Name three of the characteristics of wounding that have had an effect on your life.

3. Name some of the negative thinking patterns that you can think of that cause you to close your heart off from receiving love and giving it away.

4. Where was the place you ran to for refuge from the pain and abusive behavior unleashed on you? (Remember, some people run to worldly things to numb their pain, such as pornography, overeating, etc.)

5. George MacDonald named 12 thought patterns that comprised areas of negative thinking and darkness in a person. Which ones can you identify as a part of your life? And do you have other ones you could name?

6. Can you remember a time in your life that your pain may have caused an area of darkness; and can you forgive the one who brought the pain and shame into your life?

SAMPLE PRAYER

Father, I acknowledge that there are areas of unhealed pain in my life that have inflicted pain on other people. I ask You to show me my cycle of pain that has hurt or wounded others. I ask You to forgive me for misrepresenting Your love to others. Forgive me from living my life as a "Victim" instead of a "Victor," in Jesus' name.

Endnotes

1. This quote was accessed off of http://en.thinkexist. com/quotation/life_is_what_happens_to_you_ while_you-re_busy/171775.html on January 21, 2012.

2. George MacDonald, *Creation In Christ: Unspoken Sermons*, (Vancouver, B.C.: Regent College Publishing, 1976), 140. George MacDonald's *Unspoken Sermons* were first published in three volumes in 1870, 1885, and 1891.

Chapter 4

Breaking Free: Uprooting the Shaky Foundations of Strongholds

(Jack)

It was February of 1981. My crew of the 44-foot boat *The Life of a King* and I were off the coast of the Outer Banks when a northeast wind began to roll in. The Outer Banks is where warm water gulfstream currents always flow to the north at 3.2 knots. My crew and I had decided to ride this one out as we began to feel the motion of the boat taking on more swells. Up and down, up and down. It was better than any ride at Disney World that I had ever been on. This northeaster was causing the seas to come from the south, making ready a more violent ocean than most northeasters cause.

This part of the Outer Banks is called the graveyard of the Atlantic because it's some of the roughest ocean in the entire realm of the Atlantic Ocean. More boats have gone down there than any other region of this portion of the world. When you get caught in a northeaster on a 44-foot fiberglass boat, 30 to 40 miles from land you just cannot imagine the fear and terror. You can't imagine what it's like when the winds are howling at 50 miles an hour and every other boat has headed to safe harbor but you. You just had to catch more fish than everybody else and you had to stay out because the fish just eat it up right before the storm hits. You sit in expectation of the next great thrill of your life as you begin to watch this big, black northeaster coming in from the horizon. (It was not until later that I discovered the root issue as to why I always had to stay longer and catch more fish. It was for the praise of man, especially one man: my dad.)

The adrenalin begins to pump through your veins as you get your lines down. You begin to pull up 20- and 30-pound snapper and grouper. Sometimes they come up piggy backing and you have double the catch. You get so lost in the high. The violence of the waves against the bow of our boat makes the effort to reel the fish in a task that the weak man could not endure. Hook and line was how this boat captained by me would be bringing in their catch. We were real fishermen and real fishermen did not use electronic nets. Muscle them up and in.

I had been taught as a boy to be strong and to use my manly strength in every area of my life. Just before the northeaster struck it began to get really calm. Like the silence when the eye of a hurricane is passing over you, it hits with all of its furry and, like a freight train, the power behind this kind of wind is incredulous.

Forty- to 50-knot winds, gale force at times, begin to hit you. Within a matter of a few minutes you could be facing 15- to 25-foot seas. You look up into this wall of water at times and wonder if your boat will rise and fall without bottoming out. There is a price to pay for loading the boat up in those last couple of hours. The faint-hearted, who think they will brave a trip with Captain Blithe, usually end up tied to their bunks in fear of being washed overboard or holding on for dear life over the side of the rail throwing up all they have put into their systems over the last few meals. It is the worst possible feeling you could ever feel; worse than the worse flu you could contract.

We thought we would ride this one out. But by nine or ten o'clock that night the seas were running 15- to 18-feet high. You know that this is not as high as they could or will get. I love my 44-foot Thompson Trawler because it is made out of fiberglass with a hull that is made to set itself upright should it turn over. But when you are caught in seas like this you just can't imagine the fear and the panic when you know there's no one else out there. If anything happens, you're all alone. It got so rough that finally the weather bureau gave out warnings that any small craft still out needed to get in. It wasn't going to calm down. It was blowing 60 to 70 miles an hour by late that night.

There's a Scripture in Psalm 107 that was the first passage I ever memorized when I came to the Lord in 1980:

> *Those who go down to the sea in ships, who do business on great waters, they see the works of the Lord, and His wonders in the deep. For He commands and raises the stormy wind, which lifts up the waves of the sea. They mount up to the heavens, they go down again to the depths; their soul melts because of trouble* (Psalm 107:23-26).

The night now was pitch black with the wind blowing 40 to 50 miles an hour. The boat would rise up on the top of the wave and then come down into the trough, and all you can see is water on both sides. You know all it takes is one rogue wave: two waves come together to form a monster wave that rams into you. That one wave can sink you in seconds and no one would know where you had sunk. Literally, you would be wiped off the face of the Earth as if you had never existed. In that type of weather, in four minutes hypothermia has got you, you lose consciousness and are gone.

All I could do was just worship and pray at that time. I had just become a Christian and I was just crying out to God. But I had a crew on my boat, a few other guys that could do nothing but cry because there was no hope for them. My hope was that if we didn't survive this night, eternity would be there for me. For them, they knew where they were going. They knew what happens if we went under the water. And their soul was at their wits end. Psalm 107:27 goes on to say: *"They reel to and fro, and stagger like a drunken man, and are at their wits' end."* As night began to set in over the horizon, I knew from previous experience that this was going to be a bad night, so I hid every knife on the boat.

There is only one gun allowed on my boat, and that's in my bunk. But on nights like this I carry it under my belt because even the sanest of men become insane when facing the possibility of death. Finally my crew came to me and begged me to try to get the boat in. "We've got to try," they said. I could tell from the tones of their voices that even my most experienced deckhands had given in to the negative thoughts of "what if." No one, least of all me, wanted to die that day being known as the ones bringing in the biggest catch. I mean, would it really matter if I allowed our crisis to end our lives? No praise of man was worth that. But oh, the praise of man, if I could get this boat over the bar and into the inlet where there was safe harbor.

I knew that perhaps there was wise, sound wisdom in their request, so I gave the order to pull the anchor and get underway as we had 30 miles to run toward Ocracoke, the closest port to us.

Ocracoke Inlet has one of the most dangerous inlets on the East Coast. It's a small, narrow channel with a sand bar on the southern side and a set of rocks and jetties on the northern side. The inlet is only about ten-feet wide or deep where it comes across, which is fine in a shallow draft boat that only takes on five-foot of water. But when you rise up on the mountain and you come down to the depths, by the time that sea's gone and there's no water left on the bar.

We had to come in across that bar. When the boat in front of you goes across, you watch as it is lifted up on a wave and then slams its propellers and rudders down into the sea. It can destroy the entire propulsion system if you don't time your crossing just right and then the next wave turns you sideways. I've seen boats broach in the inlet.

When we pulled up to the inlet, the moon was shining and the sea on that other side was visible. The seas were breaking, 15-footers rolling across the bar. But our commercial boat only made six knots. There's no way to cross that bar without a wave catching you, turning you sideways, and broaching you, rolling you right over on your side. You can't imagine the nausea you feel. You know once you are on your side, a broach, there is not much chance of surviving. On the other side is safe harbor if we make it: but it's what you're going to have to face to get off of that rough ocean and get your ship into a safe port.

I told the guys that there is no way we could possibly do this. We would just get thrown around. I suggested going a few miles back offshore, and riding the storm out, waiting on the ocean to calm down a little. So we turned the boat back around and ran about a mile offshore and anchored up. The weather bureau was giving us no hope for calmer seas. They just kept saying it was going to get worse; it was going to get worse.

Fishermen are one of the hardest, toughest people you'll ever meet. There is little positive emotion, and there is no softness or tenderness. There are no tears. Commercial fishermen are an angry, rough, tough bunch of people. But that night, even with the best crew on the Atlantic Ocean, these rough and tough fishermen can fall apart like little babies crying uncontrollably, pleading with a God that they had no personal relationship with at all. Desperate men do desperate things when facing death.

As we travel the nations, bringing the message of healing and restoration, I've found that's where most people live. Just like we see in verse 26 and 27 of Psalm 107:

They mounted up to the heavens and went down to the depths; in their peril their courage melted away. They reeled and staggered like drunken men; they were at their wits' end... (Psalm 107:26-27 NIV).

It doesn't make any difference what race or social status one may have. It doesn't make any difference how long they've been Christians, or what their position is in ministry within the Body of Christ. I find that eight out of ten people live right in this place. Their whole life has been a life of pain, disappointment, anger, abandonment, and rejection. Very few have hope that they will ever, ever make it across the bar and into a place of safety.

Most people live at their wits' end.

We see them coming to this other place where they begin to cry out to the Lord in the midst of their trouble. What we've found is very few people are willing to face what it takes to cross the bar, to ride out the storm of life, their rogue wave, and have enough courage to position themselves for whatever it takes to make it to safe harbor.

It takes courage to look into the face of fear and make the choice to live and not die. It is the strongholds of our emotions that often keep us in the rough seas. Strongholds that speak to you, telling you that you will never make it.

I watched for just the right moment to position the boat so that the wave would pick up our stern and lift us up just high enough for me to steer the boat past the jetties into the inlet. It was going to be the scariest night of our lives, but if we made it we would have *bragging rights* in the bars for many nights to come.

Very few are in the position of being relationally involved with people that understand what it will take to get them across the bar. Just pray more. Just go to church more. Just do more. Just study more. And they've tried it, and yet they still find themselves a mile or two from shore with the torment of knowing that on just the other side of that sandbar lies safety. All we have to do is *face the danger of that moment—the danger of crossing the bar.*

For many of us, facing our woundedness is the most dangerous thing we've ever done. We've spent a lifetime sedating our wounds with drugs, alcohol, or with immorality. This counterfeit way of meeting needs will never bring you to a point of overcoming and being the champion you were designed to be. It is in our beginning the process that allows us to overcome and break free and discover the real heroes within ourselves. It is the process of understanding why we act the way we do (our woundedness) and dealing with our habitual behaviors, the strongholds of thinking, and acting on those thoughts of destruction.

For those of us in the Church that are really spiritual with hyper-religious activity, we try to perform enough to earn God's love. That was my life for 44 years. Doing all the right religious things, but still *not at home in love* because I was afraid to get in touch with the *hidden core of pain and the issues in my soul that were hindering me from receiving love.* The two guys that were with me on that vessel begged me, "Please, please, Jack, take us across. *We believe you can do it; you've been there before."*

Going across the bar in real life is not much different than crossing those scary seas. As I was faced with one of the most decisive moments of my life, my mind began to race back to thoughts of my family. They say that your life really does flash before you in times like this. What would happen to my family if I don't make this and we all end up dead? For a brief moment I began to ponder back on our lives together. I began to think what would I have done differently in my relating to them? It was as if a video was playing in my head, replaying my life.

Being an adventure junkie, my first 30 years of life was spent living on the water growing up in the Daytona Beach, Florida, area. I spent every day of my life as a child on the water. I was a fishing boat captain by the time I was 20 and lived from the adrenal rush of one adventurous sea event to the next.

I had met and married a wonderful girl who understood my desire for adventure and never tried to hinder me from living life to the fullest even if it meant I might die young.

Trisha, this beautiful blond, grew up in the country in Red Bank, South Carolina, with her family and extended family around her at all times. The greatest challenge she had ever faced was consenting to marry me.

That she did. I had two conditions to our marriage. The first one was that I would never marry in a church. I grew up in what I call High Church. I had received my eight-year attendance pin and never felt like I could be close to God. He was presented to me as something that you only worshiped, not someone you could relate to. Going to Catholic school did not help with my image of Him either. The nuns and their habits always frightened me. Now, I am not trying to put these denominations down, I am just explaining as a child what I was taught and what I experienced and my reaction to it.

As an older teen my parents stopped going to church and no one forced me go, which was just fine with me. So I told Trisha I would never marry in a church. She agreed to this and we married on a 65-foot fishing boat called the *Snow White 111* on the water in the inlet right outside of Ponce Inlet, Florida.

Deciding to marry in December in Florida normally should not have presented to be a problem. But for whatever reason a northeaster decided to visit our area and with it came the coldest day Floridians had seen in many years.

The next day the headlines of the local newspaper read "Jack Frost weds on Snow White Boat on the coldest day in Florida history."

I have always taken my adventure into every area of my life and my marriage would be no different.

The second condition to our marriage was that Trisha would never complain about my being on the ocean, no matter how long or in what kind of weather, and she would never try to talk me into leaving my first love!

Although I truly did love Trisha, the ocean was my Rachel and she would have to settle for being Leah or not marry me. Again, she agreed. Right here she would probably add, "What was I thinking," or "How stupid can one person be to agree to such an agreement." But again, she did. I often have wondered why; but with my understanding of strongholds and how they affect our choices, I have uncovered this mystery.

We began to date two years prior to our marriage and had broken up right before her dad died. The only reason we probably got back together was because I went up for her father's funeral and realized that I had never felt loved until I met her. Giving her up was one of the worst choices I had ever made and I wanted to experience that love again. I needed a place to attach my lifeline and she needed someone to replace the feeling of abandonment that she felt after her dad's death.

We were like two ticks without a dog. We began to suck the life right out of our relationship. Hardly did a day go by that I did not feel suffocated from her clinginess. In order to get away from her, I retreated to the ocean, leaving her daily to struggle with her feelings of abandonment. Neither of us could understand how once we were married, we no longer enjoyed the presence of one another and did not want to continue in the relationship. It was much later in life that we learned there are three great harvest times for poor behavior that we have sown earlier in our lives: your wedding day, the birth of your first child, and your children growing up and becoming teens themselves.

Teaching on strongholds and the effect they can have on us after many years and how they can endanger relationships had not been introduced to our world yet.

In fact, it would be years of pain and damage before we could come to a place of understanding all of life's circumstances that entangled our life together. Whether or not we would make it was anybody's guess. Neither of us thought we would and we were ready for divorce.

We had decided that our marriage had failed and were on the verge of giving up when life began to take us on an adventure to discover why we did the hurtful things we did to each other.

Time passed by quickly as we spent day after day in a miserable relationship with nowhere to go for help. By this time I had left the sea and was in full-time ministry. We thought we were the only ones in leadership who had problems in their relationship, so in order to keep our status we continued on in our very dysfunctional relationship until Trisha decided she could no longer be a hypocrite. Her heart continued to harden toward me until one day our pastor's wife noticed and, along with our pastor, confronted her unhappiness by asking me what I had done.

If my wife was so unhappy, as the head of the household, it was my responsibility to fix it. So I set out on another great adventure that took me to many places and caused me to read many *how-to* books. *One thing I have learned is that if the so called "how-to" books don't deal with the issues of your heart, then their information is just that—information.*

Then someone told me how being wounded in earlier relationships can cause us to develop habit patterns of thinking and strongholds, which can cause behavioral problems that affect our lives so no sort of lasting change occurs in us.

Teaching on being wounded and strongholds, those deceiving lies that I embraced as truth and allowed to become habit patterns of my flesh, those very habits were what directed how my relationship with Trisha and the kids was going to go.

Acting out those strongholds revealed areas of woundedness that caused me to kick into self-preservation mode. These behaviors were seeded so deep into my heart that they became a part of my personality. This person was not at all who I wanted to be or was designed to be.

As my pastors confronted me, my first thought was, "She ought to just get over herself." I mean she is married to a good man who has never cheated on her, but I did have my "mistresses." One was the sea, then later I exchanged her for the *mistress of ministry.* The foundation of both was a stronghold of thinking that sent the message to anyone around me that what I considered the most important thing is the most important thing, and if you don't agree with me and can't make me look good, then to heck with you. I had no value for anyone who couldn't do and live my way.

Habit structures of thoughts, strongholds of thinking that are motivated by selfish ambition, have at the root of them the ability to destroy relationships. Habitual thinking patterns that say, "If you don't think and act like me, then you are wrong, making you the problem," are a great example of selfish expectations. As long as, in my heart, I continued to making Trisha's needs a problem for my life, then it was just a matter of time before our relationship would die. I had to find a new way of thinking that included her needs being a priority in my heart.

But time is a terrible thing to waste and I was wasting my time on how she could serve me. I even told her once that I wished she would be more like women of old that served their husbands and made his needs their purpose in life, much like Charles Wesley's wife. I even went so far as to give her an example of a minister's wife who met her husband at the door each night with a pan of water to wash the cares of the day off of him. I told her the least she could do when I was home was act as if nothing mattered to her but me. I came very close to handing her a prison ministry *as I could see the look of murder in her eyes.*

These were strongholds, negative patterns of thinking that bring destruction to your relationships. They build this structural fortress of thought that has to be torn down to their very foundation with their root system pulled out. Jeremiah 1:10-11—uproot, tear down, destroy, overthrow, then build and plant.

Strongholds have strong foundations. When a house is built on a strong foundation, it will be difficult to tear it down.

As you look at the common ways strongholds are built into the structure of a person's mind and then how they seep into their heart, it will be easier to identify them and begin the process of uprooting and tearing them down so you can build and plant *strongholds of love.*

COMMON WAYS STRONGHOLDS ARE BUILT

Strongholds can be passed down from generation to generation through the iniquities of our forefathers.

When we allow negative strongholds of thinking to cause us to make choices that wound our families, these choices can become sin or a lean toward sin that can be passed down to other generations. This is why the Bible talks about God visiting the iniquity of the fathers on the children, and on the third and fourth generations of those who hate Him (see Exod. 20:5; 34:7; Num. 14:18).

I can already hear what some of you might be thinking. This is Old Testament stuff. Jesus died for all of that. Positionally, you are correct. But how many people do you know that, when they became born again, change their old habit patterns immediately? This is why Paul spoke to us about the renewing of the mind (see Rom. 12:2). Once I identify these old habit patterns and strongholds of thinking, I can take them to the cross of Jesus and deal with them there.

Every act of obedience upon our part is an inheritance to our children. So too they may also inherit every act of disobedience. Every choice we make to walk in darkness influences our children—this means that every act of disobedience also has influence. Many times strongholds are built within us from just living in our father's house. There may have been no apparent wounding, yet we find ourselves living in the same destructive lifestyles of our fathers later in adult years. How many of you know alcoholic people who grew up in alcoholic homes? Did their alcoholic parents cause them to become alcoholics themselves? No one can make you become like your examples in life except for you. The choices are yours. Did growing up in that environment influence or cause you to have a lean, an iniquity, toward alcohol? I would be willing to say yes since statistics would back me up. That is just one of many examples of a later discussion of some principles that Trisha and I have discovered on laws to relationships.

Strongholds can be built from deep hurts that resulted from wounds we received.

A broken spirit dries the bones (Proverbs 17:22b).

Our past experiences with relationships have caused us to draw conclusions about life. These relationships may shape our value system (what we see as right or wrong). They may determine how we interact with people or even with God. They may distort the way we relate to our families. We may begin to see life and others through the lens of how we were treated in our past. We don't need to spend much time in the past, but we do need to understand what may be a root issue as to why we act the way we act today with the goal in mind that our *past no longer should dictate our future.*

Refusing to allow a platform where people can deal with their struggles and habit patterns of negative thinking keeps people locked up inside. They are told that as a new creature in Christ they should just get over themselves. This will cause confusion to the person who is really trying to deal with their behaviors and strongholds, especially if one of them is seeking praise from man because this need was never met in childhood.

Now you can tell them that it all was handled at the cross and they should no longer struggle with their habits. Yet they still do and become quickly frustrated and give up on any type of changed behavior that actually will cause them to be a better person. Hopelessness sets in as they make choices to give up. This happened to me with many well-meaning Christians in my life. It was not until I came across teaching on strongholds and my own revelation of unconditional love that combined with my habit pattern of changing behaviors. When they did change, when I chose to deal with my strongholds of thinking, understanding that I am loved no matter what, it was then that my relationship with my wife and family changed. (Read my book *Experiencing Father's Embrace*.)

Strongholds can be built within us through a misrepresentation of love—how we perceive love or rejection.

We were created in God's image. God is love. God is light. God is a relational being. We too were created for love and relationships. We were created for love to flow through every fiber of our being. We have been destined to receive love so that we spend our lives giving love away to others.

If we have been a victim of a misrepresentation of love, it often leaves a wound. Often parents express their love by the things they do for us and not by heartfelt expressed love given through words, tones of voice, and touch. This can leave a hidden anger within a person because they feel they have not been given the love they were created to receive, thus creating a love deficit. It has the potential of distorting our view of authority figures in our lives or our view of Father God.

A great example of this is a father who shows his love by working two jobs to provide for his family, but the child interprets this as a lack of love because little one-on-one time was given to the child and the father was often absent for special occasions.

Strongholds can be built within us by judgments or the inner vows we make toward others, God, or ourselves.

This call also be stated as, I will never treat my child the way my parents treated me.

Whenever you judge another person out of a deep wound or disappointment, it always comes back to you in one form or another. It is the law of sowing and reaping. Whatsoever a man sows that shall he also reap (see Gal. 6:7-9). "For every action there is an equal and opposite reaction." (We will see this in more detail a little later.)

Here is an example: perhaps you were hurt deeply by a girlfriend or boyfriend and said to yourself, "I'll never let anyone hurt me like that again." Then you feel yourself hardening your heart toward all men or women later in life. This can overflow into your relationship with your spouse.

Strongholds can be built within us through the words that people speak over us.

There is something very soft and tender inside of a person that can be pierced by words. The author of Proverbs knew the power of our words as it led him to pen, *"Death and life are in the power of the tongue, and those who love it will eat its fruit"* (Prov. 18:21).

Words can be like railroad tracks that we seem destined to follow our entire lives. Words can affect us for years to come. If we believe in the prophetic words and those words affecting us for years to come, then why do we find it difficult to believe that negative words spoken into an unhealed heart can also have an effect on us and our outcome? No one wants this to be true, but we have seen it too many times in the people we have ministered to.

Again, it goes back to telling a person a lie long enough and they believe it. If we are told every day that we don't finish things or that we are clumsy or put your own word curses here, we tend to follow those words, especially if someone in authority in our lives, like our parents, has spoken them.

A friend of ours was told all of her life that she was clumsy, disoriented, and ditzy. She honestly came across that way, until she found out the meaning of her name. Her name is Crystal. Crystal means "brilliantly clear." She forgave those who spoke the other things over her, she embraced what her name meant, and she no longer struggles with the confusion she used to have.

Strongholds can be built within us through false doctrine or false teaching.

Any teaching that does not represent the Spirit of Christ can become a corporate stronghold. A corporate stronghold is a way of thinking, feeling, or acting that a group accepts as truth. It is built within people one thought at a time until lies or deception become truth to them. They often become a hiding place for demonic oppression.

The Spirit of Christ is grace, mercy, compassion, love, meekness, and lowliness of heart. Christ brings comfort by expressing value to a person. You don't have to do it right all of the time to be loved and honored by Christ. While not condoning sin, Jesus let people know that Father was never angry with them because of their sin. Father loves us the way we are and, because of this great love, we are motivated for change.

Strongholds can be built within us through our ethnic or cultural backgrounds.

Corporate strongholds exist in every culture or ethnic group. They develop over a period of time from a practiced belief or tradition that has been around for ages. People accept that this is the way they are and feel there is not possibility of change. We must ask ourselves, "Is this personality or character trait like our forefathers and countrymen, or is it like Christ?"

Here are a few examples of this:

- Americans pride themselves on their independence. This has overflowed into our relationships with God and each other. We tend to feel we don't need help or anyone in our lives. In fact, my family lives in the "Independent County of Horry," a double whammy for us.

- In Asian cultures people are often extremely performance-oriented. The Japanese may be one of the most performance-oriented cultures on Earth. (This was told to me by a Japanese minister I met in Toronto.)

- Europeans can tend to be very reserved in giving expressed love and affection toward their children. This is especially true of the Scandinavian countries.

Strongholds are reinforced through our false belief structures.

For as he thinks in his heart, so is he (Proverbs 23:7).

For the thing I greatly feared has come upon me, and what I dreaded has happened to me (Job 3:25).

Positive thoughts are associated with God and negative thoughts with satan. What we believe about ourselves is our truth even if it is a lie. When we allow the accuser to bring our thoughts into self-condemnation and self-judgment, then our emotions will follow our thinking like a caboose follows the engine of a train. If our emotions and thinking remain negative, then it will affect how we view life, treat others, and the way we feel about ourselves.

We have also seen this overflow into people's health. Our bodies respond to what we tell them the same way they respond to what we physically feed them. By feeding them lots of fat and sugar, the body will shut down as it responds to what we are putting into it. Feed your mind negative thoughts on a consistent basis and your mind will send a message to your body to respond in like manner.

Examples include:

- If we think long enough that we have no value and self-worth, then we will "sell ourselves short," treat ourselves cheaply, and the way we feel will be affected. Thus addictions, self-abuse, or sexual promiscuity can result.

- If we believe that no one loves or cares about us, then we draw rejection out of people. People end up treating us like we feel about ourselves. Depression and hidden death wishes can result.

- If we continue to think life is too painful to live and that we just want to go on to be with Jesus, our body can respond to the thoughts of death, and sickness sets in.

Everything dies when we don't feed it. If we can develop a habit of not feeding our negative thoughts and strongholds, they will die. How often do you hear the saying, "All hell has just broken loose"? I want to challenge us to change that belief to, *"All Heaven is breaking loose!"*

QUESTIONS TO PONDER

1. Who in your life have you hurt and wounded from unhealed hurts of your past that have caused you to think and believe lies about how you relate to them?

2. What are the support structures that give life to your own habit patterns of flesh that wound those in your life?

3. What lies have you embraced from word curses that have set you upon your own destination to destruction?

SAMPLE PRAYER

Father, I desire to be more like You. I desire that Your power and presence would reveal to me everything that I've hidden from You. I pray that You would help me to see where I've built up strongholds in my life, help me to see the ways I've made my reality truth, and the way You are always present with me to help me overcome those obstacles.

Forgive me for building strongholds that block me from You. Forgive me for treating my reality as truth, and not what You say as truth. Forgive me for believing my circumstances more than Your revelation.

Lord, I don't need another "how-to" book. I need You! I need the power of Your Spirit and a revelation of Your love in my heart. I need You to come and remove the veil that has been over my eyes, and help me to see how I've erected strongholds in my relationship with You, my friends, and with my family. Give me the power and the grace to overcome those obstacles. Give me the love to conquer all. In Jesus' name, amen.

Chapter 5

Getting Across the Bar by Discovering the Laws of Relationship

(Jack and Trisha)

Then they cry out to the Lord in their trouble, and He brings them out of their distresses. He calms the storm, so that its waves are still. Then they are glad because they are quiet; so He guides them to their desired haven. Oh, that men would give thanks to the Lord for His goodness, and for His wonderful works to the children of men! Let them exalt Him also in the assembly of the people, and praise Him in the company of the elders (Psalm 107:28-32).

The decision was made that we would take the risk. Crossing the bar, as scary as this might be, was a better choice than staying stuck in a rough ocean. Sometimes, when we are faced with a life situation where there seems to be no *easy way out*, we have to choose the path of courage in order to find our way through, or as in our case, the way to the other side of the bar where we were assured of a safe haven with our community of like-minded guys, the fishermen.

I would have to admit that I had been there before. I did have the skills to get us across the bar that night. It would not come without dealing with fear and embracing courage. *Courage is not the absence of fear.* Courage is just making a choice to face our adversity and deal with it face to face. We were looking deep into the face of our adversity, fully afraid of what lies ahead, but making a choice to go for it anyway.

Waiting for the right wave in the right moment is exhilarating. You have to be precise in your positioning or you will make the boat broach, turning it up on its side and losing everything on board. The draft of the boat sinking can also cause anything close enough to be sucked under as she goes down. The only other scenario is that she will right herself, but you lose your catch. Choosing to head across the bar was not just about our safety, but also about not losing thousands of dollars as we watched our fish tanks lose our cargo. You never wanted to come in with a *broker*. You had to at least pay for the expenses.

"Batten down the hatches and get ready for the greatest thrill of your life," I told the crew as some of them tied themselves down and others just hung on for dear life. Then came the wave we were looking for. For a brief second I stood in awe of her, knowing she had the power to save us or kill us. To me this was an awesome revelation as I waited for her to pick us up and make her choice.

The wave thrust us right between the jetties and the sandbar, and for a brief moment flipped us onto our side. I was thrown across the deck as she flipped, but was quickly able to get up and get back to the wheel as she bopped herself upright. This 44-foot Thompson Trawler was true to her reputation that night.

We were able to take the boat right across the bar, moved it into calm water, pulled a little bit over into Pantego Sound, about a half mile to the south of Ocracoke Harbor where 50 vessels had come in earlier and were tied up.

The crew was already on the side of the boat, letting go of their lunch and dinner and everything else, myself included. All I could do was go into a safe place outside and just let it all go because of the fear of that moment. For the first time in my life I was speechless; the confidence I felt, the peace of knowing we had survived another day when we should have all perished. But did I take the time to give honor to the One that saved us or was I relishing in the praise of man as we began the half hour trip down the waterway getting ready to pull into Ocracoke Harbor at 2 A.M.?

More than 50 fisherman and the bar employees came out to greet us when they heard the roar from our engine as we pulled into the harbor where the once great sea pirate, Black Beard, tied his vessel up, having actually lived in this area. They could not believe that any vessel had been left in the horror of the raging storm that night, a storm that later was tagged as one of the worst northeasters in the history of that area.

The fishermen had been up all night partying during the storm as is often done while waiting on these types of storms to blow over. Heavy winded storms are usually gone in a day and you can return to some of the greatest fishing as the fish rise closer to the surface to find food. It was a hardy group of tall-tale mariners; most so drunk they could hardly throw the lines to us. I began to notice all the looks of astonishment as they stared at us, wondering a question that they all knew the answer to. Finally, one of the more sober ones called out, "Did you cross the Okracoke Bar tonight in this weather? Are you mad, my dear Captain?" By now the crew had gotten over their fear, and there was a pride filling them as they stuck their chests out and said, "Yeah." Then another drunken sailor hollered out, "I wouldn't have crossed that G-d bar in a battleship." (Now don't get offended here, this was the language of the culture of fisherman.)

My crew then had a story to tell! They had no clue that there was a moral to the story. They just wanted the bragging rights they felt they had earned that horrible night. The lesson they did not seem to understand was when you're willing to face a lifetime of hurt and pain, when you're willing to risk being led across the bar (facing your crisis) in what may be one of the most dangerous moments or seasons of your life, in that moment, when you discover the pain and other sins against you have built up to the max, and perhaps your sins against others have left so much shame and woundedness, that is when Jesus wants to lead you. That's when He wants to make you a witness to His power and His love and set you free.

This kind of experience in Christ is not for the faint at heart, just like crossing the bar that night took courage from that rag-tailed group of burned out humans who run to the sea to escape their lives of pain. It takes a person who has come to the end of himself and is willing to take a risk as they deal with the pain of life. *When our pain outweighs our shame, then and only then will we change.* A friend of mine, Roger Gosnell, told me this.

I believe that as we change our course now and begin to look more into the area of the cause, it is going to take us deeper into this journey that we have begun in the earlier chapters of this book.

Now it is time for the *ME Examine*. If you want bragging rights, a testimony of a healed and transformed life that will bring healing to your family and your sphere of influence, we have to look a little deeper into woundedness for freedom. We will need a closer look that will take you to a place of change as you examine yourself without becoming a victim in the process. A friend of mine, Doug Murrell, published on his Facebook page, "Change is in the air because the pain of staying the same is more than I can bear."

And Jesus said:

> *For a good tree does not bear bad fruit, nor does a bad tree bear good fruit. For every tree is known by its own fruit. For men do not gather figs from thorns, nor do they gather grapes from a bramble bush. A good man out of the good treasure of his heart brings forth good; and an evil man out of the evil treasure of his heart brings forth evil. For out of the abundance of the heart his mouth speaks* (Luke 6:43-45).

I love what John Sandford says: "Good fruit, good root; bad fruit, bad root."[1] What John is saying here is that we need to identify our cycle of pain that causes us to continue with behavioral patterns that wound others. Not just the cycle, but also the power that fuels the cycle and then produces the woundedness in our relationships that cause them to be unhealthy. This is the bad fruit we are talking about.

Our oldest son Micah developed a heart of justice. I am not sure if he was born with it or not, but I think it probably began to manifest in his life from sources of wounding that he received from us, his parents. Out of all of your children, your firstborn is usually your laboratory where you experiment with raising your children with your concept of parenting.

"That's just not fair," was what we often heard Micah respond if we disciplined him with harshness. Unfortunately for Micah, we had not received a revelation of love during his formative years, so he was corrected out of what we felt was right and fair, never listening to or valuing his opinion on the subject. "Well, life is not always fair, Micah. Deal with it and do as I say, not as I do," was the response of two unhealed hearts. Micah began to judge us in his heart and would become angry when we tried to discipline our other children without using the same method of harsh and wounding tactics we used with him. Micah built his own fortresses of thought here; he began to believe life was unfair, so it became his responsibility to make it fair in his sphere of influence.

There are more details to this, but for now let me just say that we have had to ask all of our children to forgive us for our wounding of them. We ask them to also forgive us of our past that caused us to treat them without honor and respect.[2]

This sense of what is right and fair can be useful when the bitterroot structure behind it is identified and dealt with. Micah judged us with his own concept of justice, which was birthed out of his anger toward us. Once he dealt with the anger and forgave us, his sense of justice began to work for him.

Today my son is a South Carolina State Trooper, given the authority to carry out the laws of the highways and also the laws of our land. He does this treating people with honor and respect as he helps them to understand these laws. If you were caught speeding, Micah would love to help you understand that you don't speed in the Horry County area without a consequence. He has made many "new friends" by helping people understand the laws for a safe highway experience in the Myrtle Beach area.

Like it or not, there are laws to healthy relationships. When these laws are broken, then there are also consequences that you can either allow to change who you are, thus producing what we call good fruit, or you can choose not to and produce the consequences of what we call bad fruit, unhealthy relationships.

THE FOUR LAWS TO RELATIONSHIPS

The Law of Honoring our Parents

Children, obey your parents in the Lord, for this is right. "Honor your father and mother," which is the first commandment with promise: "that it may be well with you and you may live long on the earth" (Ephesians 6:1-3).

This law states that in every way we honor our parents, blessing comes to our lives. *Honor* means to have respect and value for a person, even if we do not agree with his or her behavior. To treat someone as ordinary is to dishonor them. But what if the opposite happens? What if, in our heart, there is resentment and bitterness toward them? For every action there is an equal and opposite reaction, and law is set into motion.

"Then God said, 'Let the earth bring forth grass, the herb that yields seed, and the fruit tree that yields fruit according to its kind, whose seed is in itself, on the earth'; and it was so" (Gen. 1:11). Pears always produce pears. Wheat always

produces wheat. In whatever area you did not honor your parents, in that very same area you may find yourself having problems as an adult or in your own family. It is law!

You might say you have no conscious memory of dishonoring your parents, but remember that thoughts lie, feelings lie, and emotions lie. The only truth in our lives is the fruit of our lives, what we produce through our influence, whether good or bad. What good or bad are you producing in your relationship with family, friends, or peers? You know the tree by the fruit it bears (see Matt. 12:33).

The Law of Judging

Do not judge, or you too will be judged. For in the same way you judge others, you will be judged, and with the measure you use, it will be measured to you (Matthew 7:1-2 NIV).

Judgment is when we judge others out of a wound or out of feelings of rejection. If, in our heart, there is blame, condemnation, jealousy, envy, unrighteousness, anger, bitterness, or unforgiveness, then this can be judgment. It sets into motion God's unchangeable laws. We must ask ourselves, "Do we judge by the fruit of the Spirit or by the deeds of the flesh?"

Law demands that we judge another (for every action, there is an equal and opposite reaction), so judgment must come back to us. It is not God judging us but the law.

When we judge another person for the wrongs done to us, then we are demanding payment for those wrongs. If we want justice, then the same rules apply to us. We cannot ask for mercy for ourselves and judgment for others who have wronged us.

Kay Lewis, a friend and co-worker at Shiloh Place Ministries said, "You will never inherit what you demand."

The Law of Sowing and Reaping

Do not be deceived, God is not mocked; for whatever a man sows, that he will also reap. For he who sows to his flesh will of the flesh reap corruption, but he who sows to the Spirit will of the Spirit reap everlasting life (Galatians 6:7-8).

They sow the wind, and reap the whirlwind… (Hosea 8:7).

Every good deed we sow will eventually reap blessing. But every deed sown in dishonor or judgment will also reap seed after its kind. It is law, not God's judgment on us. And we always reap more than we sow.

The Law for Becoming What We Judge in Others

Therefore you are inexcusable, O man, whoever you are who judge, for in whatever you judge another you condemn yourself; for you who judge practice the same things (Romans 2:1).

It would be helpful to read Romans 2:1-16. In verse 12: *"For as many as have sinned without law will also perish without law; and as many as have sinned in the law will be judged in the law."*

When we judge another person with negative emotions and allow it to take root in us, eventually it may bring forth a harvest of the same behavior being found in our lives, the life of our spouse, or in the lives of our children.

So many of us have said, "I will never raise my children the way my parents raised me," only to find themselves doing many of the same things they judged to be their parents' faults and weaknesses!

The little boy in the closet vowed in his heart that he would never hurt his children through alcohol the way his parents had wounded him. This choice, if made without hatred or bitterness toward a person, will stop a generation from becoming the next generation of alcoholics. But when this is birthed out of anger, hatred, and bitterness over pain experienced as a small child, then the vow can only produce seed after its own kind.

Shirley became an alcoholic from the woundedness of her past. It was how she chose to deal with her personal pain. Jack judged his mom out of hatred for her, for how she wounded him and became an alcoholic and drug addict from the wounding of his past. The result was cause and effect according to the law of sowing and reaping, and the law of becoming what you judge in another. Jack sowed hatred toward his parents and became what he hated in them, plus more. Did his parents cause this in his life? The law caused it. His parents contributed to his pain, but the law caused the pain of his choices.

There are laws in the natural that keep things in natural order and likewise there are laws in the spiritual realm that keep things in order there.

Newton's third Law of Motion says: "For every action there is an equal and opposite reaction." Thus, if your action is to jump off a cliff you will drop to the bottom of that cliff…reaction. Law will pull you downward…it is law. The law of gravity also applies here…law demands. Did the law cause you to jump off the cliff? No, your choices did.

Broken laws in relationships can cause strongholds to run deep within us because it is often difficult for us to admit we are still hurt or angry inside, or that we still carry resentments. Our loyalty to ourselves or to our parents prevents us from seeing the roots. But there is no escape from law, other than the power of the cross.

Christ redeemed us from the curse of the law, having become a curse for us... (Galatians 3:13).

Without repentance, broken laws become the hidden energy source that drives our fleshly behavior patterns! Satan takes advantage of the broken law by imposing a curse.

QUESTIONS TO PONDER

1. Are you duplicating things in your life that you resented in your parents or someone else—character traits, actions, emotional patterns, motives, or attitudes?

2. Can you specify what from whom?

3. Has the Holy Spirit been working on you in an area of your life, but you seem powerless to overcome it? Does there seem to be a driving force behind it that you have no control over?

SAMPLE PRAYER

Father, I ask You to forgive me for judging (put a person here—usually a mom or dad) for her (behavior). I made a vow out of anger and pain that

I would never treat anyone the way she treated me. I ask You to forgive me for that judgment. I ask You to help me view that person with Your eyes and Your heart toward them. I ask You to come and heal their pain and my pain as I bring this judgment to the cross.

I ask You Holy Spirit to cause the storms of our life to be stilled as I put my trust in You. I ask You to guide my way out of this sea of pain from broken relationships and I thank You for getting me unstuck. I thank You Jesus for Your blood that brings healing to our emotions.

Endnotes

1. John Sandford often says this in his teaching seminars he does across the country. He is a motivational speaker on topics of inner healing. He can be reached at Elijah House Ministries in Spokane, Washington, or Post Falls, Idaho.

2. See the series by Jack Frost on *Healing the Hearts of Your Family,* available at Shiloh Place Ministries' website: http://www.shilohplace.org/.

Chapter 6

Breaking Free From Shame Through Understanding the Causes of Being Wounded

(Jack and Trisha)

"And you call yourself a Christian…" Those were the words from the glaring hatred that Smut, my best deckhand, had just spoken to me. "You wonder why nobody wants to talk to you at the bar or ever wants to hear anything about this so called Jesus you have found. Well, I am going to tell you why!"

I remember it was about a year after I (Jack) had been born again. And I was one of the harshest taskmasters that the sea had ever seen. I was called Captain Blithe not only behind my back but also now to my face. I was a rage-aholic, a screamer, and I was almost impossible to live with during that time at sea. I had this radical born-again experience in February 1980 that set me free of 10 years of drug addiction, 11 or 12 years of alcoholism, and 15 years of pornography. I had the most radical salvation experience. I don't know many people who were as saved as I had been.

Treating people with respect and honor was not a part of the package of the salvation experience. It would be years before I would learn the concepts of John 13:34-35: *"A new commandment I give to you, that you love one another; as I have loved you, that you also love one another. By this all will know that you are My disciples, if you have love for one another."*

You see the most *natural thing on Earth ought to be for us to receive love and in turn give it away.* It's what we were created for. It's our destiny. But even though we've been born again, it's not always that easy, is it? I mean the giving away of unconditional love. If Smut hadn't lost that fish, I wouldn't have screamed at him. He made me do it.

Out of our mouth come the issues of the mind or the emotions. I feel that the issues of our mind and emotions come from the causes of the woundedness that have built the strongholds of thinking that keep us locked into the old habit patterns of our flesh. Good fruit, good root. Bad fruit, bad root. There are still issues in our life that misrepresent the Father's love. Second Corinthians 10:4 describes how strongholds exalt themselves above the *"knowledge of God."* We have been told all of our Christian experience that God loves us. Why do we continue to act the way we do when the Bible tells us over and over again we are loved? It is those strongholds, those habit patterns of thought, that are the cause behind our woundedness that has exalted itself above the knowledge of love.

At the moment of salvation old things have passed away. And Second Corinthians 5:17 says all things have become new. But in our mind, will, and emotions there can still be root systems or ungodly beliefs. All it takes is someone in your life to become Miracle Grow fertilizer for you. Have you noticed it's usually your wife or your husband? Have you noticed what a gift of God your spouse is to you to help you find the unyielded areas of your heart?

Rick Howard, a teacher and great theologian from the San Francisco Bay, Redwood City area, tells the story of someone flying across a desert in Africa. Out in the middle of the desert, where there was just white sand as far as you could see, he looked out the window of the airplane and saw a green spot out in the middle of the desert. They flew right over it, and he looked down and there was this jungle, perfectly square, right in the middle of the desert. He called the stewardess over and asked what a jungle was doing out in the middle of the desert, and she told him the government was drilling for oil and struck an underground river. As an experiment they thought they would see what happens if the water was turned on. So they put in a one-square mile sprinkler system as an experiment, didn't plant any seed—just turned the water on. Out of a place that had been totally dead for thousands of years with no life sprung a jungle, and this from seed that had been planted a long time ago.

Your life can be going rather well and then out of the blue, crisis hits. And in one moment of crisis, things you thought had died to you long ago are suddenly there raising their ugly head and the fire-breathing dragon just burns everybody to a crisp.

Isn't that a lot like you and I? When someone comes along and provokes or waters our dry areas, then life begins to grow again. Now, depending on the level of healing we have had in our woundedness will determine the amount of growth. But this could be positive also. If I have an area of dryness that needs some spiritual watering, and someone who has a measure of healing comes along and spends time helping me, new life will grow when it is planted in good strongholds.

See, the cross of Jesus Christ has provided a way for us to die to these old root patterns and systems that may have been building in our life from generation to generation. We have the choice to water with life-giving elements, or the choice to water the dry areas that bring about death.

Jesus said, *"Every plan which My heavenly Father has not planted will be uprooted"* (Matt. 15:13).

Dealing with the causes of being wounded is, in my opinion, the way to give Father the permission to root up life-bearing plants that produce negative fruit in our lives. This takes us back to cause and effect, not blame for the mistakes of our life and the wounds that we have brought into our relationships. John Burroughs once said, "A man can fail many times, but he isn't a failure until he begins to blame someone else."[1]

Paul understood this and said it this way:

If, then, I do what I will not to do, I agree with the law that it is good. But now, it is no longer I who do it, but sin that dwells in me. For I know that in me (that is, in my flesh) nothing good dwells; for to will is present with me, but how to perform what is good I do not find. For the good that I will to do, I do not do; but the evil I will not to do, that I practice. Now if I do what I will not to do, it is no longer I who do it, but sin that dwells in me (Romans 7:16-20).

That passage began to set me free because my biggest battle has been with aggressive striving, tremendous intensity, and task orientation that always dishonors and devalues.

Out of the wounds I felt I had received from my performance-driven parents, I developed a stronghold of thinking that I have to do it better than everybody else and nobody can do it good enough for me. This was the message sent to me by my parents and this is the message I have sent to my family. I never realized that this kind of thinking creates an environment where children feel they have to earn your love in order to feel they have any value in your heart.

If my children did not do things exactly the way I expected, then I would scream at them, saying words like: "You stupid idiot, can't you do anything right? Dummy, who showed you how to cut the grass? You never finish anything you start. If you can't do a job right then, for Pete's sake, don't do it at all!" I thought I was training my children how to take responsibility and do things right. I never realized that I was releasing word curses over them that would follow them around causing them pain.

They began to conform to the very words I had spoken over them which caused them to close their hearts off to my love. They embraced the lie that *you can never please him, so why bother trying?* This left them with feelings of shame. *Shame says you're a mistake, not that you have made a mistake.*

When I would do the things I didn't want to do, I thought that was me. That I was broken! I identified myself as that person, and I constantly lived in the state of self-condemnation and self-judgment. I seemed powerless to love, especially my family.

In the beginning of my experiencing Father's love, I was taught the Word that says I'm no longer the one doing it but it is sin that still dwells in my heart. When God looks at me, He's not looking at me through the behavior of that aggressive striving and devaluing that I often inflicted upon others.

Now Smut saw it, and he didn't want the Gospel that I represented. I'm thankful to say, though I have misrepresented God's love for the first few years at sea, many of the fishermen have come to the Lord as I found God's love. As I began to be able to acknowledge the sinful areas of my life and the misrepresentations of God's love, and to be real and open and not act perfect or be demeaning toward them, they began to desire the very thing that set me free. We've seen them up and down the East Coast coming to the Lord, some of the hardest core commercial fishermen alive.

The apostle Paul relates to this when he asks, "Who's going to set me free from this issue in my soul, this sin that is present in my soul?" (See Romans 7:24).

I think healing from the wounds that we allow to become our strongholds of thoughts, our habit structure of the flesh, is twofold.

First and foremost, *we need a supernatural breaking forth of the love and power of God in our lives.* Living as a Christian example in the world cannot be done without Him and His daily presence. Otherwise, we truly are living a performance-based lifestyle.

If you live from your identity, and how good you feel about yourself is being met based on your performance, you will demand that from others as well. Living here can also cause you to become very independent because you don't need anyone but yourself to have a successful life.

The second answer for healing is *being able to identify the cause of the wounding.* In doing this you are better equipped to understand and face the pain, forgive the one who wounded you, and position yourself for a supernatural encounter with Him.

Let me say that He loves you no matter what! This is our position as a new creation in Him. It is because of the price He paid at the cross for us and our sin. But there is still a need in the life of most Christians for the renewing of our minds. We stand a better chance of being *unbound* if we understand the hindrances

Part of dismantling the stronghold is identifying the cause of the wounding. There can be *many causes for wounding.*

Divorce

- Produces insecurity and fear in a child
- Children suffer rejection from the parent who leaves
- Children receive rejection from the remaining parent
- Produces a negative self-image that can cause shame
- Causes difficulty in bonding
- Causes fears of abandonment and rejection
- Children often blame themselves for divorce

Children of Alcoholics

- A breakdown of communication occurs
- Emotional needs aren't being met
- Children think alcohol is more valuable than they are

- Fears and insecurities fill their heart
- Children often find it difficult to emotionally bond with others
- Children may become independent and self-sufficient

Performance-Oriented Home

- A home with high standards has no room for failure
- Rigid exterior rules without intimate relationship: this will breed rebellion
- High standards are not tempered with enough expressed love and affection
- Leaves a child performing for love and acceptance
- Can impart fear, insecurity, and emptiness

Abusive Parents (Unloving or Harsh Discipline)

- May be experienced in emotional, physical, verbal, or sexual abuse
- Silence always speaks rejection in discipline
- Withholding expressed affection
- Source of great inner pain
- Cause feelings of guilt, worthlessness, and shame
- Cause repressed anger

- Getting close to God means being punished again

- Destroy a child's sense of worth and cause him to lose motivation in life

Passive Father and Dominant Mother

- Father assumes you know he loves you so rarely speaks it. You don't feel his love, so it creates an emotional vacuum in the child's heart. You begin to believe God is like that, that He is passive. He does not know how to care for your needs.

- Doesn't appear to be home even when he is home

- Dominant mother is not in line with God's divine order so there is silent rebellion released in the home

- Can defile the sexuality of the children as they begin to seek wrong answers for right needs

Being an Unwanted Child During Pregnancy

- Most unwanted children suffer from rejection

- Babies born during depression years often become the highest rate of people who suffer with depression

- Being a "wrong sex" baby may leave a wound

- Adopted children often have a wound of abandonment

- Mother is a communicator of well-being. She can communicate love or rejection; she can communicate her own oppression, fears, and insecurities

One Child in a Family Receives an Unfair Measure of Love or Attention While Another Does Not

- Can leave a child feeling like a second-rate child
- Leaves suppressed anger or rage
- Can leave an adult feeling like God loves others but not himself/herself

Death of a Parent can Leave a Wound of Abandonment

- Possibly produces hidden anger against loved one for dying
- Possibly influences the person to blame God for the death
- Person may blame themselves for death

Children Who are Denied Expressed Love and Affection

- May grow insecure and wounded in heart
- Have difficulty giving or receiving love in adult years
- Suffer with depression in adult years

- Have frequent illnesses
- End up striving and performing in order to receive love

Authoritarian Fathers

- Have a need for attention and focus on themselves
- Major in rules and truth, but are empty of ability to love
- Don't allow child to develop their own identity
- Try to live their life through the child
- Not interested in the goals or interests of the child
- Child may begin to see God the same way

Negative Words Spoken by Parents

- Dummy; stupid; you'll never make anything of yourself—such words act as a word curse for a child and cause the child to conform to the words spoken. The child believes the lie, and words are like "railroad tracks" which they may follow the rest of their lives (see Prov. 18:8).

Rejection by Peers

- Can cause a child to be independent and isolate himself/herself from others
- Hinders their ability to bond or trust in the adult years

Rejection by Boyfriends or Girlfriends

- Person may make inner vows such as, "I'll never let someone hurt me like that again."

Rejection Within the Church

- Can cause a person to judge God or all Christians by the woundings of immature and carnal Christians
- Usually takes two years to get over a church hurt

Rejection by a Spouse

- Often leaves a person feeling like a failure
- Leaves behind bitterness and resentments
- May leave a person feeling like they aren't good enough to be loved

Wounding can cause us to start compacting our hurts, emotions, and feelings. Usually by adulthood, the areas in which we have stuffed our pain begin to leak out in our relationships and personality. You, your family, or others you are in relationship with begin to see the characteristics of your woundedness.

Some of the characteristics of wounding are:

- Withdrawal or isolation, which controls your relationships
- Walls of self-protection; causes a fear of man, thus producing a lack of trust for people

- Possessiveness; bonding to only a couple of people and becoming threatened when others try to befriend them

- Emotionally dependent relationships

- Difficulty in receiving correction or instruction

- In constant need of attention

- You feel unloved so you draw rejection out of other people

- Self-centeredness or victim mentality

- Emotionally immature

- Pattern of broken relationships

- Judgmental attitude

- Lack intimacy with God and see Him as distant

- Stress related diseases

- Argumentative and quick-tempered

- Self-rejection, no self-worth

This is our experience in Christ. In Him, we are being transformed every day *"by the renewing of our mind"* (Rom. 12:2) and the *"renewing of the spirit of our mind"* (Eph. 4:23). We must daily *"lay aside the old self"* and *"put on the new self, which in the likeness of God has been created in righteousness and holiness of the truth"* (Eph. 4:22-24).

In other words, we must die daily to anything within us that is not like Christ. As we understand the cause of our wounds we are able to work through our processes and become *unbound to life entanglements.*

If we choose to sow to the flesh by allowing our fleshly responses from wounding to dwell within our soul, then we begin reaping what we sow. Many people will say this is God's judgment. That just is not so. *Law polices itself by us judging ourselves with our own actions.* Thus, we eventually get our identity from those we have not fully forgiven. That is enough judgment and causes us to dwell in darkness.

But Father has promised us:

Instead of your shame you will have a double portion, and instead of humiliation they will shout for joy over their portion. Therefore they will possess a double portion in their land, everlasting joy will be theirs (Isaiah 61:7).

QUESTIONS TO PONDER

1. Can you list three of the most destructive characteristics of wounding that you are presently dealing with?

2. Did you need to ask someone to forgive you for responding to them out of your woundedness?

3. If you answered yes to the above question, who are the ones that come to mind?

SAMPLE PRAYER

Father, I choose to forgive (put the names here) for wounding me so. I have responded in un-Christlike ways in my heart. Forgive me for responding to others with (name the wound). I thank You for the blood of Jesus, and by that blood I forgive and release the person who wounded me. I ask forgiveness for my responding to them with destructive behavior. I ask for the character and nature of Christ to replace this destructive habit pattern that cause me to wound others. Thank you, Lord. In Jesus' name, amen.

Scriptures that might help to understand this process are:

- Second Corinthians 10:4-6
- Ephesians 4:22-24
- First Corinthians 15:31

Endnote

1. This quote was accessed off http://www.brainy quote.com/quotes/authors/j/john_burroughs.html on January 23, 2012.

Chapter 7

Breaking Free From an Expectation of an Unhappy Life and Breaking Forth Into New Planes of Purpose

(Trisha)

The Eastern Seaboard of the U.S.A. is breathtaking during the winter. The waves are rolling in with just enough of a chop to produce whitecaps on the very top of each wave. To a sailor this is God's creation at its finest, but to a person who rarely even goes to the beach, the ocean was a raging sea.

Watching this on our trip around the Southern Keys of Florida reminded me of earlier times working in the snack bar on a party fishing boat and making fun of all the people who would get sick before we even left the inlet. I loved this…the more people we could get sick, the sooner the boat would return to the dock, and we all would get to go home early without losing any pay.

I remember all the times in our early years of marriage that I spent caught in storms working with Jack on his fishing vessel. Although I never had been seasick, I have often come pretty close, especially when you have to watch others throw up their breakfast and *you are one of the ones who gets to clean up the messes that others make.* I guess over the years my life has not changed much in that area.

In your early 20s, experiences like this are some of the greatest times in life. You think you are invincible and life will always look and feel this way. Watching those waves white cap did not have the same effect on me that day some 30 years later, but I could watch the look on Jack's face and know they were sending a different message to him.

Rest, rest, rest. All we could think about was finally taking a sabbatical. For the next several weeks there were no e-mails, no travel, no kids, and no problems. Or so we thought.

Rest means different things to different people.

We had been given this trip of a lifetime to celebrate the ten-year anniversary of this great ministry, Shiloh Place, which had truly been built from scratch. It was also our anniversary. I was glad to have this time where I felt like I would have Jack all to myself. No one else pulling on him for time, ideas, or ministry; so I agreed to this cruise knowing that for Jack the ocean was a refuge where he could find the well-needed rest that both of us needed.

The ministry had become visible and Jack was very much in demand on the *Father Loves You* circuit of speakers. Our testimony not only had brought change to our family, but it was bringing change to the world around us and to nations all over.

We never dreamed of the ministry becoming so successful from just two people trying to make better choices so that their family could live healthy lives. But thanks to God for the revival that happened in Toronto. Those choices of change and their testimony was reaching the far corners of the globe. Every day people came from places I had never heard of just to have a few moments with a couple who had changed so much that their kids actually loved them.

The phones never stopped ringing. Since I believed in being home with my children while they were small, Jack would whisk off to anywhere. He was invited to conferences with the faith that more healing and change would occur.

Our vision was to provide a place in the Body of Christ where pastors could come either alone or with their *leaders (influencers of people)* and real change could occur. It was lasting change that would be taken first into the homes of these leaders and from there to the world. We have learned that a healthy pastor does not always guarantee a healthy church, but an unhealthy pastor or leadership team always guarantees an unhealthy church. The knowledge of the statistics of pastors leaving the ministry daily (over 50 percent of pastors leave the ministry within the first five years of becoming a pastor) causes us, a couple of burned out pastors in earlier years, to have a deep sense of compassion for leaders. We never realized how truly devastating their pain was until becoming involved in their lives.

I am always amazed at the pain I see in leaders. Leaders who are full of zeal and passion, and over the course of the battle of bringing wholeness to their towns, give out.

It was exhilarating watching many of these leaders personally come to us or to one of our events to hear our testimony and see our changed lives. It gave them hope to pursue change for themselves that would change their family and their spheres of influence. I love watching people do a metaphoric change right before me.

Carrying that much pain and empathy had taken its toll on us mentally and physically; we needed some rest. Years ago we had learned the value of taking those mini-sabbaticals to other ministries for encouragement so we could always deal with any issues that we did not see but were bringing pain to each other.

This was going to be our trip of a lifetime. We both were looking forward to our two-week cruise and time exploring the Keys. We were going to swim with the dolphins, ride in a submarine, fish all day, and cruise for two weeks. Who would not have been excited over this?

"Trisha, Trisha, can you hear me?" Jack was sitting beside me with his hand on my leg as I shook violently. Neither of us knew what was happening to me and I was afraid to move. For the next few hours what the doctor would later call physiological seizures would stop and then begin again. Physiological seizures are seizures that occur in the body while your mind is fully aware of what is going on. What was happening to me? Fear gripped my heart as the shaking became more intense. There were breaks here and there, but then they would start back again. The intensity of fearful thoughts was almost more than I could mentally stand. Was I having a stroke that would cause me to become a crippled, handicapped person for the rest of my life?

I refused to go to a hospital in an unfamiliar town and begged Jack to take me home. At first he refused, dreading a 17-hour drive with me shaking violently. "Oh, just go get on the boat, things will be fine once we are on the boat," was the idea he had. I could not believe the lack of judgment he used in that moment and it was not until weeks later that we uncovered the real reasons behind his insensitivity to my crisis.

He was a desperate man for rest. He knew just how badly his body, soul, and spirit had become out of tune with his relationship with this new loving Father he had recently discovered. And he wanted to get back to that place of "being at home in love."

Confused and disappointed, Jack made the phone calls to cancel our place on the ship and all of the fun stuff, and we packed the car to go home. Silence, dead silence. The only communication we had over the next 12 hours were the sounds of my thrashing when one of the seizures would overtake me.

I so needed to feel comforted by Jack, but Jack had to deal with his own emotional response to the disappointment at the loss of rest. Whose need should have been more important? Mine, was my thinking. I could be left this way for the rest of my life. But Jack was physically and mentally in the same shape as I was myself. He just did not shake. Silently, I was the source of his frustration and, as hard as he tried not to blame me, I could feel this coming from him. All it did for me was to add shame on top of what I was already dealing with.

The next day the doctors did not have a clue what was happening to me. So I self-diagnosed my condition and found out that I had lost my ability to cope. Menopausal women can lose a hormone that sends the message to your brain that you are safe. When that happens, all the symptoms that I was experiencing can happen in a person's body.

My situation sent my doctors on a quest for answers. Unfortunately, back then the only answer was to treat this condition with tranquilizers and pray for this hormone to restore itself. It took exactly two years, but my coping hormone returned and I never had one of those seizures again.

This event in our life left me feeling like I no longer had value in Jack's heart. Oh, I knew he loved me, but something was different in our relationship. "Not again," was all I could think. Not another season of being alienated from each other; just when we were at the best place we had ever been with our family and especially with each other.

Had the Father's love message really been real? I mean my image of who He was in my life had so drastically changed. I was now also traveling, taking this message to the world.

I had come to another crossroad of having to make a choice. I could choose to allow my situation to revisit old strongholds, those habit patterns of thinking that brought comfort to my flesh, or I could choose to remember who He is and always has been in my life. Always, when I choose to trust Him, the plan has an awesome outcome. It's not always the outcome that I like, but it is always the best outcome—and time proves it to be true. I have so much lemonade!

I chose the latter and thank God that I did. Who would have known what my future was going to look like just a few short years later. I wanted to make choices that would make my relationship with Jack iron clad. When you don't know what to do, the best thing I can think of is to set out to find where Jesus stands in the situation. Where He is will reveal an answer that brings you to a place of peace in your heart.

Now don't confuse peace with passivity. I have usually had to fight a battle to find and keep peace. Even though the battle can be intense, I am the victor in Christ. You don't always believe that when you begin a journey to a new phase with Him. Does it ever stop…is there ever a place where you can just be done with all battles? Ask King David. David should have been in the heat of the battle fighting alongside his men, but for some reason was at home. He was not sick, nor was he in any way unable for the battle; he was not in need of rest during this time, he was just at home instead of where he was supposed to be during this season of his life.

I wonder what would have happened if David had been in the battle with Uriah instead of where he was (see 2 Sam. 11).

Being in a place of resistance in our lives can often have the consequence of opening doors to sin. Too many times in my life I have made the wrong choice, in wanting my flesh to be the one who was comforted. This time I really wanted to view our pain from Jack's point of view, instead of just my own.

So a road trip. At the time I had no idea that this trip would be the last time that we would go somewhere to deal with our relational pain. It was time for a road trip back to the panhandle of Florida to some of the most beautiful beaches in the world. The beaches of Destin, Florida, are absolutely one of the most serene places I have ever encountered.

We met this strange little couple that would be the catalyst to bring this last phase of healing into our relationship. Truly, like the angel who told Joshua, "I am not for you or against you; I am on the side of the Lord" (see Josh. 5:14), Betsy and Chester Kylstra were on the side of the Lord. They helped us to look at the emotional impasse that Jack and I had come to.

Again, you might ask the question, "How can this couple that had experienced so much healing in their relationship, this couple who had this dramatic encounter with love, still be dealing with issues?"

I am one who believes that as long as we live, if we are making a difference in the world through the example of our life, there will always be more to learn about ourself and those we are in relationship with. I do believe you come to a place where you allow the Holy Spirit such access to you that you don't want to wound anyone, but instead want to truly be that mirror image of Him.

I think Jack and I had reached this place. We went to the Kylstras with the motive, "Father, help me to love the other one more. Show me the other one's perspective so that I might truly love like You." I wanted to know why my illness wounded Jack so deeply.

It was not me at all. It was his need for rest. It was rest that eluded this man for much of his life; rest that brought him to the place of knowing that no matter what, he was loved and had value. Jack was on a quest for this place that, if found, would have brought his body, soul, and spirit into perfect harmony.

In this harmonious place, nothing matters more than receiving His love and, when necessary, giving it away through His presence within. This place of total submission that we at that time believed many people had a struggle finding.

I was able to see Jack's pain and his great need for rest. I was able to take a good look at all of my ungodly beliefs that hindered his total discovery of finding this place. Was I causing Jack not to find this? Of course not. *Remember, no one can create your spirit, they just reveal it.* But we can be a part of the effect that relational indifferences have on each other. Once you take blame out of a situation, you also remove the shame that is involved. You come to a place of wanting the other one's needs met before yours. This is true love. And in finding true love, we find rest.

Jack discovered this place in the Father's embrace because he never stopped looking. He never gave up on love. He never stopped giving away the love he found to his family first.

He died. He died leaving us a legacy to continue in the wake of.

The hardest thing for me since Jack's death has been learning how to be happy again. When you are removed from a person who was one of the greatest sources of life and happiness, it leaves a black hole in the heart that nothing seems to fill.

I love my children and grandchildren, but even the joy of watching them fulfill their dreams and destinies, watching and loving every cute, identifying thing your grandchildren do that makes them cuter, smarter, sweeter, and just more loveable to you than anybody else's grandchildren still does not fill that void, that hole. I never thought about how deeply the union of two people becoming one really is.

You do not plan to be the one left. Silly as it might sound, Jack and I used to joke about who would go first. Now that we had the answer to that question, I had some hard choices to make. I would either make those choices from the pain of my past or I had the opportunity to now remember who my Father really is and break free of the past inability to trust the most important male figures in my life.

I did not want this habit pattern of thinking to prevent me any longer from totally trusting in my Father God. I knew I still had purpose and my destiny was unfulfilled. But life seemed hopeless without Jack and even more so with the ability to trust in Father God. I had to, once and for all, break free of this mental stronghold. *In order to break free and become unbound to a life of hurt and woundedness, I had to learn to face my enemy. I needed to name it so I could effectively take ownership of my behavior in order to rid my life of the mind games a stronghold can have on me.*

Who my hero would be now depended on choices I would make from a heart in the process of being healed, or the choices would come from a wounded heart and soul.

Demolishing the old habit patterns of thinking, those strongholds that kept me bound, seemed like an endless process. Do they ever end? For me many have, but there are times that satan, being who he is, wants to make sure those that can and will make a difference are stopped. Jesus died for our past and has forgotten. Knowing this is truth has not stopped satan from trying to keep me bound to my past. Paul understood this and wrote a huge part of the New Testament on the renewing of the mind.

Every cell in our body has memory. Being put in the right situation can cause the memory of the pain of our hurt to revisit us. Do I spend most of my life in the drudgery of sitting and thinking about those things? No! But I am familiar with pain and how to deal with old patterns when they try to remind me of old hurts.

Let's look at it this way. Some months back I had a conflict with a past employee. I was right; I felt they knew I was right. In my opinion they tried to cover up their actions by gathering people around them and trying to turn others against me. You know it is always easier to blame the boss. The employee left, but for months afterward, when someone mentioned their name, I had to fight joining into negative conversation about them. This employee had pretended to be my friend and what they did really hurt me. I guess the boss is never supposed to have feelings. Even though I overcame this in my flesh, it was another story in my mind. We ran in the same friendship circles, so we would often run into each other. You could just feel the tension and the mind games that were going on. Finally, neither of us was willing to give up our mutual friends so we met with each other. I am excited to say we both took responsibility for how we hurt the other one. Now when I see this person, I actually see the great gift of God that this person is to the Body of Christ. I don't struggle with the mind games any more, but I did when I was placed in the right situation with them. Even though I had long since dealt with the sin of the wounds that I had inflicted as this person had, we still had to renew our minds with what the Word says about loving others. I admit I did not like this person, and only just recently can honestly look at them with love.

My old habit pattern of thinking that I really can't trust people had raised its ugly head, even though I knew Jesus had redeemed me from those old habit patterns. The sin attached to it was repented of and covered by His blood, but memory and pain need time and processing for healing to occur. I don't by any means advocate spending a lifetime on one's pain, but if we can help people understand their wounding and teach them that it is OK to renew their minds daily, then the time for the healing process is lessened.

I get a little feisty with people who never spend time understanding the pain of others, so they judge people by their experience. *Don't **should** on someone.* Well you *should* move on; you *should* stop dwelling on your past; you *should* understand you are a new creature in Christ. Although those things are very true, pain is also very real. If you did not grow up in an abusive environment where your image of God is seen through the lens of your earthy parents, then it might be hard for you to have compassion on someone who needs a little more understanding of everything that Jesus died for.

Putting your experience somewhere else may cause them a lifetime of shame and guilt as they think something must be wrong with them because they are not like you. Never tell a person to just get over it or put their past behind them. Some people need help to do this. I am one of those who did so that today I can help others understand the process of Jeremiah 1:10-11.

For years I listened to many of the fathers of the Faith Movement. I heard those wonderful messages of prosperity, healing, and the Kingdom, and I loved them all. But as a new Christian I became so frustrated with the idea that these messages weren't working for me. Did God love those guys more? Then I saw this Scripture and received my answer. There is a process to building faith. Jeremiah tells us to uproot, tear down, destroy, overthrow, and to build and plant (see Jer. 1:10-11).

I got it. I was building a faith message on top of old beliefs, strongholds, and habit patterns that had not been uprooted, torn down, destroyed, and overthrown. The whole process of demolishing strongholds begins with this verse.

So how do we demolish strongholds in our lives? This is the answer we all have been waiting for.

Healing will never bypass the cross. The cross is our balancing stick for all teaching on healing. This is the purpose of Jesus dying.

I have never believed that Jesus' death on the cross was just a one-time price for everybody at the same time. What I mean by that is Jesus only had to go to the cross once, but not all of us have gotten saved at the same time, nor have we been hurt in the same ways at the same times. We do not all get revelation at the same time. You can always go to the cross. Jesus also died for the sins I will commit tomorrow. I am not going to set out to sin, but I am so thankful that if I should wound someone tomorrow, there is forgiveness for me through the process of my working out my strongholds.

There are three requirements for healing:

1. You must hurt enough that you have no choice but to change.

2. You must learn enough that you have hope for change.

3. You must receive enough unconditional love that you are motivated toward change.

And there are two roads the Christian may travel for change to occur:

1. The Jericho Road: the road of supernatural miraculous intervention and healing.

2. The Calvary Road: renewing the mind and the spirit of the mind.

And do not be conformed to this world, but be transformed by the renewing of your mind, that you may prove what is that good and acceptable and perfect will of God (Romans 12:2).

That you put off, concerning your former conduct, that old man which grows corrupt according to the deceitful lusts, and be renewed in the spirit of your mind, and that you put on the new man which was created according to God, in true righteousness and holiness (Ephesians 4:22-24).

The Calvary road experience demolished strongholds by taking off one layer of thought at a time (similar to the layers of an onion). The greatest hindrance to this healing process will be the original sin of pride.

Andrew Murray writes:

All desires to be loved, all indifference to others' needs and feelings, all sharp and hasty judgments and utterances, all manifestations of temper, all touchiness and irritations, all feelings of bitterness, and all feelings of separation and isolation have their root in pride because pride ever seeks itself![1]

Pride sees the wrongs that others have committed but never identifies or empathizes with others' hurts, wounds, and weaknesses. Pride usually admits no wrong. Pride hates to take responsibility for its own mistakes. Pride justifies its negative attitudes by its desire to totally be right.

Pride produces a heart that is hard, that is self-sufficient, and self-dependent. Pride is more interested in being right than doing right. Pride blames God and other people when things go wrong. Pride excuses and justifies its bitterness and resentments.

Pride is the greatest hindrance to bringing down fleshly strongholds.

We are not held accountable or responsible for the wounding that others have brought into our lives. We are held responsible for the way we have reacted to the wounding. It has been our choice to respond in the judgmental ways of pride.

WE DEMOLISH OUR STRONGHOLDS BY

Confessing our sin.

If we confess our sins, He is faithful and just to forgive us our sins and to cleanse us from all unrighteousness (1 John 1:9).

Acknowledge destructive behavior patterns as sin.

But now, it is no longer I who do it, but sin that dwells in me (Romans 7:17).

List the negative thoughts and emotional patterns and see them for what they are. They are your fleshly responses to the wounding. If that characteristic in your life is not like Christ or the fruit of the Spirit, it is sin.

Identify the root cause behind the negative behavior as sin. Ask yourself, "Where did that behavior come from? Who treated me that way? Who hurt me like that? Whom have I judged, thus releasing the curse back into my life?"

Confession of sin sometimes needs to involve another person you trust.

Therefore confess your sins to each other and pray for each other so that you may be healed (James 5:16 NIV).

For if we would judge ourselves, we would not be judged (1 Corinthians 11:31).

The first time we confess our sin, God forgives. But often we need to confess daily in order to cleanse the wound. We do this so that the destructive fruit and negative patterns begin to whither and die.

The scary thing here is in the telling someone of our sin. Why should I have to do that? I would feel ashamed. When you make yourself accountable to others for your sin, then the enemy does not have a hold on your flesh. Satan traffics in darkness and hidden places. Without those places in our lives, sin has nowhere to hide. Any hidden sin or undealt with areas are darkness and make us want to hide. When we humble ourselves and deal with sin, we choose light over darkness.

Darkness may mean these things:

1. Unconfessed Sin:

When I kept silent about my sin, my body wasted away through my groaning all day long. For day and night Your hand was heavy upon me; my vitality was drained away as with the fever heat of summer. I acknowledged my sin to You, and my iniquity I did not hide; I said, "I will confess my transgressions to the Lord"; and You forgave the guilt of my sin (Psalm 32:3-5 NASB).

2. Broken Relationships:

If we walk in the light as He Himself is in the light, we have fellowship with one another....But he who hates his brother is in darkness and walks in darkness, and does not know where he is going, because the darkness had blinded his eyes (1 John 1:7; 2:11).

3. Walls of Self-Protection:

Then the eyes of both of them were opened, and they knew that they were naked; and they sewed fig leaves together and made themselves loin coverings. And they heard the sound of the Lord God walking in the garden in the cool of the day, and the man and his wife hid themselves. And he said, "I heard the sound of Thee in the garden, and I was afraid because I was naked, so I hid myself" (Genesis 3:7-10).

In my past I have dealt with three areas of sin in confession:

- Secret Sin: these are the negative and sinful thoughts that we quite often have.

- Individual Sin: this is sin we commit against each other.

- Corporate Sin: this is the sin we commit against a family or group.

It was in hating the sin or habit structure that I began to love who I am in Christ. This began the process of leading me into repentance. *"Abhor what is evil. Cling to what is good"* (Rom. 12:9).

EMBRACE A REPENTANT ATTITUDE

Produce fruit in keeping with repentance (Matthew 3:8 NIV).

Repentance always involves action. It is not just emotions and tears. It is to be so grieved at the wounding and grief, that our actions and attitudes bring to others and to God, letting them know we will do whatever it takes to heal their wounded hearts.

Seek to become *ripe* (ready). Ripeness is a willingness to stop putting the blame on others for causing us to react in such negative ways. It is to stop justifying our behavior and attitudes by focusing the spotlight on someone else or their negative behavior. *People don't create your spirit, they reveal it! "The goodness of God leads you to repentance"* (Rom. 2:4). *When the sense of His presence is near, repentance becomes part of our character.*

Repentance also involves guarding our words.

For out of the abundance of the heart the mouth speaks…For by your words you will be justified, and by your words you will be condemned (Matthew 12:34,37).

And the tongue is a fire, a world of iniquity. The tongue is so set among our members that it defiles the whole body, and sets on fire the course of nature; and it is set on fire by hell (James 3:6).

The more conversation that is given to an offense or hurt, the more energy and life we give to the hurt. It can cut off the flow of repentance. We end up stimulating one another with the offense. We must practice a daily discipline of not speaking of the hurt or offense. We must only speak of the offense with someone we trust, who will make us judge our own motives and attitudes.

GIVE AND RECEIVE FORGIVENESS

And whenever you stand praying, if you have anything against anyone, forgive him, that your Father in heaven may also forgive you your trespasses. But if you do not forgive, neither will your Father in heaven forgive your trespasses (Mark 11:25-26).

Forgiveness is not a matter between you and someone else. It is a matter between you and God. You don't forgive someone for his or her own sake. You forgive them for your sake so that you can get your identity from God and not from the one who hurt you.

Our greatest example for forgiving others, especially when we were not in the wrong, is Jesus. He prayed, *"Father, forgive them, for they do not know what they do"* (Luke 23:34).

I love to speculate when I read the Word. Not to change the meaning, but I love to pretend I am there with the person who is speaking so I can hear their tone of voice and see their body language in order to really get a feel for what the person is trying to communicate. When Jesus uses the word *Father* in the Bible, I can just imagine how

He communicates with such tones of honor and respect for Him. Jesus knows what the Father is capable of. If you are a person of justice, then you know that Jesus at any point could have changed the scenario for all of us. But He chose to bear our sin so we could be redeemed and our outcome changed from them. He agreed to live with the consequences of our sins. Forgiveness comes with a large price tag.

Jesus spoke forgiveness into us when He uttered that statement upon the cross. Two things we might want to understand about this are:

1. They don't know what they are doing (see Luke 23:34).

Hurt people hurt people. That is all most hurt people understand. They have been wounded and have developed a personality of wounding others by the examples they've seen. People give to you what was given to them. Loved people love people. I love to judge people by what they really are capable of rather than the wounding that they display from an unhealed character. I love to see the end of who they can become. Jesus forgave people because He could look at the root cause behind their destructive behavior. He could see them as wounded warriors for the Kingdom and so He treated people from this objective. He did not give them what they deserved, but died for a better outcome for them.

2. Father, forgive them (see Luke 23:34).

The key to forgiving the unforgivable lies is acknowledging our unforgiveness, bitterness, and hatred, and that we don't know how to forgive. Confess that as a sin. Ask the

Lord to forgive the offender through you. He has given you the free gift of forgiveness. Now give to another what was not yours in the first place.

FORGIVENESS IS TWOFOLD

1. We must forgive others for the hurt they have brought to us.

2. We must receive God's forgiveness for judging others, for breaking laws of relationships, and for holding unforgiveness and bitterness toward others.

Forgiveness releases us from getting our identity from our hurts and from those who have hurt us. It releases God's healing to flow through us. Then the Spirit is released to impart the Father's personality, character, and feelings in us!

Embrace the purpose behind God's desire to heal and transform us. Healing is not complete until the deserts and wildernesses of our lives are transformed into satan's greatest defeats. When we overcome a behavior or stronghold of thinking that wounds another, it becomes our testimony of victory. Our victories become a testimonial in our lives of change. This testimony of success releases around us the Spirit of prophecy and gives us the ability to help others overcome their pain.

The testimonies that still come into our ministry about the healing others have received, the marriages restored, and the families who actually like each other again simply because Jack and I decided to stop the cycle of pain in our own family, never cease to amaze me.

When I think the way the Father thinks, especially about me, I am amazed at how two average people, one from Red Bank, South Carolina, and the other from Daytona Beach, Florida, could have been chosen to express Him to the world. It really is a mind-blowing experience. It all started with *forgiveness,* then went to our desire to demolish anything in our lives that hindered us from *living Him.*

Healing takes your greatest shame and then anoints you to minister to others in the very areas you have hurt! It doesn't do away with your memories, but it changes what you do with those memories. It transforms death experiences to life experiences!

> *But as for you, you meant evil against me; but God meant it for good, in order to bring about as it is this day, to save many people alive* (Genesis 50:20).

When attacks or hurts come our way, we will seek the Father to come and comfort our wounded hearts. As Father brings comfort and healing, then we will use the very thing that was meant for evil and turn it into the greatest victories for the Kingdom of God.

Healing is complete when our destructive behavioral patterns have been transformed to caring for others when they hurt.

Taking personal responsibility for your reactions to the pain of wrongs done to you is the first step toward demolishing strongholds. You do this through the cross; by confessing your sins so that you might be healed.

Personally, I think it is up to God which process He will choose once you have surrendered control.

He made you. He sees the attitudes of your heart and knows more about the how than you could ever imagine.

I love how God, being immutable and unchanging, comes up with some of the greatest ideas for our healing that usually involve change.

QUESTIONS TO PONDER

1. Can you identify a stronghold (a way of thinking) in your own life that you thought you had overcome?

2. How has this habit pattern of thinking or stronghold wounded those that you care about during this season of your life?

3. Can you remember an incident of wounding in your own life that could have been the place where you seeded negative thinking?

4. Can you go back to that hurt, invite Jesus into your pain, and give Him permission to touch the pain?

5. Can you forgive those who have been the source of your woundedness?

SAMPLE PRAYER

Father, I come to You in Jesus' name and I give the Holy Spirit permission to reveal any hurtful behaviors or strongholds of thinking in me (see Ps. 139:23).

I invite You Jesus to reveal the source of the woundedness in my life. (Wait on a memory to come to mind; for me it was a vivid picture of being in the back of the station wagon, not feeling that anyone would comfort me by meeting my needs.)

Father, I choose to forgive those who let me down. (For me I had to forgive my dad for abandonment even before he died.)

I realize that out of my pain, my loss, or my disappointment, I have judged You and the way in which You treat or respond to me or my needs personally.

I ask You to forgive me for judging You for (whatever the lack or woundedness or need not being met was; my prayer was for not healing my dad when I needed him most). I ask You to forgive me for developing a stronghold of thinking (name the thought or habit pattern of thinking; for me it was the inability to trust) that I cannot trust You. I choose to forgive (put the person here who let you down or wounded you) for abandoning me and for letting me down when I needed him most. Father, this has caused me not to be able to trust others, so therefore I have become an untrustworthy person myself.

I break free of these entanglements by embracing the forgiveness that the blood of Jesus provided for me on the cross. I choose to develop a new habit pattern of thinking that will cause me to trust You and Your plan for my life, including the people You now place in my life for me to trust and depend on.

I ask You to demolish every stronghold that I have embraced through the wounding caused by others' pain in my life.

Thank You, Father.

Endnote

1. Andrew Murray, *Humility: The Beauty of Holiness,* (New York: Anson D.F. Randolph & Co.).

Chapter 8

Breaking Free to Finish Well or to Start Again

(Trisha)

"Trisha, I am sorry for your loss." For three hours I heard this over and over again as kind people waited to just offer their condolences to us as a family. Friends and family had come and gone for the celebration of Jack's life. Now it was the aftermath of the last 13 months, which felt like a whirlwind, that we were left to deal with. Let me say here that I would give even more than I did if it would have saved Jack's life. He was a man to be honored for how he changed and loved his family!

Where does time go? How does it pass by so quickly? How do you grieve? Do I even want to go through the grieving process? It seemed to me like a waste of good time and energy. I knew where Jack was and what I had to do in order to move forward.

It was very comforting to have such close family, friends, and a great church to help me walk through the process. I thought that life would continue on and it would not be a very hard transition to move into.

Once you watch someone suffer, even though you love them tremendously, it is almost a relief when they are no longer suffering.

Jack was experiencing his heavenly Father's embrace. I thought his destiny on this Earth was over. Boy, was I ever wrong about that one.

I would miss him terribly as I began the process of life without him. Jack's last words to me were, "Trisha, there is a Niagara Falls within you waiting to come out. Look for it, even if you feel that it is tarrying, *Wait*! You will know when to begin again." I think Jack knew he was going to die and wanted to bless me without putting fear into my heart that his earthly life was coming to an end. He knew he would not be raised from the dead.

However, much had to be done, and, as always, I would move forward with my circumstances and handle it. I was no stranger to transition. Life with a sea captain had helped me understand this.

Immediately, plans were made to move forward with the ministry as my board met and decided to make me lifetime president. Our associates had been a tremendous support to the ministry during our life crisis. Let me say right here a huge thank you to Mark and Jane Burlinson for their leadership, support, and help in navigating the first year of transition. Your grace for my lack of direction in crisis will always be remembered and spoken of when your name is mentioned at Shiloh Place.

What is it supposed to look like now? There were so many unanswered questions. I kept trying to speculate instead of just listening. Most of the employees had left to move on to different things for the next season of their lives. Who could blame them?

Everything I tried seemed to fail. I am a verbal processor and I drove people around me crazy as I constantly thought out loud. I felt like I had a safe environment to do this, never realizing that I was causing confusion amongst my staff.

I lost all sense of direction even with a vision still in front of me. If my board and family had not been there to support me, I think I would have given up and tried to find a good job and let the vision die, especially my part. I felt so broken. There is a secular song by the Goo Goo Dolls called "Iris." One of the verses of the song says, "When everything is made to be broken, I just want you to know who I am." I am not normally into a lot of secular music, but this made sense to me. I was broken and I needed to know who He is.

Bill Johnson says in his teaching, "The Responsibility of Blessing,"[1] that there are times in a son or daughter's life when you can lose the sense of His presence. He never leaves you, but the sense or feeling Him seems to have been withdrawn. In those times He wants you to dig deep to find what He has already deposited there.

In my mind this is a long process—the digging to find I mean. I know He has deposited great things within me, things others could see more than I could.

My pursuit of Him during the season of transition was going to be a great adventure. I am used to it and up for that the challenge. That is and was my life with Jack, moving from one great adventure to the next. I was pumped by the exhilarating idea that we were moving forward.

It sounds exciting, but *moving forward sometimes requires no movement.* Learning the art of really being still requires more than just soaking for an hour. It may be days or months of positioning yourself for His voice to be heard, truly being still.

Feeling like I was drowning, I finally heard what I felt like He was saying to me. After months of screaming at Him, "I don't know," became, "I give up," then onto, "I don't care!" I woke up one morning to the words, *"I am bringing you into a season of separation so I can enhance your destination."*

At this point I was wondering what else was going to be taken from me. With Jack now gone, so many of my friends, employees, and team members also left. Support dwindled even though I was traveling and working just as hard as Jack ever did while living the message. I really believed in the message we lived, but obstacle after obstacle continued to be thrown at us. Yet the testimonies continued pouring in of families being restored and changed lives all around the world from people who had either read our books, had come to our schools after Jack's death, or had come to events where I continued to share our message.

That next season was a time of letting go of all I had known so that I could be.

Our family has always been a family that is consistently moving forward to the next level of change. The process is often hard and there is usually an easier way if we skip a part of the process because it seems too painful. We are not permitted by our Father to do this, so we wait for the vision. We will wait even if it tarries (see Hab. 2:3-4).

Why? Because there is a word in this verse *chayah*, a Hebrew word that means "life." In the language of the country of Zimbabwe it means "to strike the air with life."[2]

From that time until now, I have received word after word about life and living. I have lived through the season of feeling abandoned and abused. I was not even sure I wanted to live anymore. I really felt I was done with life and

I blamed ministry for it all until one morning the word I woke up with was *chayah*, to live. I got up and put on a new CD by Brian and Jenn Johnson, entitled *Here is Love*, and I declared with a loud voice as I struck the air with life!!! I wanted to live no matter what my situation at that moment was. I knew it was going to be better.

My daughter Sarah had a three-legged cat. The cat had found her way to our interns' house. Immediately, the interns called Sarah because she is a huge animal advocate and has a way with animals much like the famed Dog Whisperer, Cesar Milan.

This poor frightened cat was abused, deformed, and full of fear with a mangled leg. Sarah decided to take her home and nurture her back to health, so she named her Zoe, which means life.

Zoe was pregnant and near death because someone decided to use her in order to vent his or her negative emotional behaviors of anger. Needless to say, Zoe did not trust anyone around her, but she still had physical needs that had to be met in order for her to remain alive. In allowing Sarah to meet those needs, Zoe has tolerated Sarah's advances of unconditional love. Zoe has never had to change in any way for Sarah and her husband Doug to provide for her needs, but through them she has seen unconditional love and acceptance and has moved closer to being able to trust again. She has gone from being an orphan living in the pit of abuse to finding her way into a palace of unconditional love and acceptance. For Zoe, it is a place of real contentment and complacency. Doug and Sarah have taken Zoe as far as their experience will allow them, so what is next for her?

As I write the last chapter to this book, Zoe is on her way to California to live with Beni Johnson in a community of believers who have created a culture for supernatural events becoming natural. I am sure there will be more opportunities for Zoe to learn trust. But Zoe will have to continue to make choices to live in order to go to the next level of life God has purposed for this cat. I think she is going to get back all that has been taken from her. I also think she is going to learn to be able to trust humans again.

I never cease to be amazed at the goodness of our Father. Without any more shame, at times I wonder why I can't see the outcome or end result the way He does. I would love to be able to live my life through His eyes.

"Swim, you can do it."

"Jack, stop the canoe and let me get in."

"No Trisha, you can make it. There is a reason for you to swim! Do you love me, Trisha?"

"Of course I do, Jack," but in my head I was planning on how to send him to Heaven before he actually went.

"Well if you love me, will you trust me?" Now this was another matter. If I still have battles with any emotion in my life it would be with totally trusting, even with people I care dearly about.

I have learned one thing about trust that I try to remember when I am faced with a new opportunity to make choices that concern this issue in my life. When *Christians don't trust God, it's because they don't know they are loved by Him.*

This is always the question that satan wants to tempt you with in times of crisis. If he can get you to second-guess your intimate relationship with Father God, then he knows it will become easier to tempt you in other areas of your flesh. It is called the lust of the heart. It can be an evil thing. Father created us to use our emotion of passion, but when we give into our flesh, passion can become lust.

"Trisha you have to trust me with this. It concerns the future." I was actually dreaming but it seemed so real. The dream continued with Jack taking me on a picnic to this camp where we were staying. On the other side of the lake was an island that was isolated from the rest of the lake. Jack had fixed this amazing picnic and rented a canoe, these were the type of dates that I enjoyed. I would much rather have these types of dates than go to the most expensive bistro in any country we have ever been to.

While on this island enjoying our lunch of fried chicken and white bread, which is something that neither of us had eaten in years, we noticed that people were screaming and an ambulance had arrived on the scene. We decided we should go and see what was going on and if we could help. While I packed up the picnic items, Jack untied our canoe and pushed it off the bank, just far enough that I could not get into it.

I asked him to come closer to the bank and he informed me that I had to swim back to shore. I can swim but did not think I could make the quarter mile swim back to the camp. Feeling myself getting a little irritated at his behavior, I asked him again to bring the boat back close enough to get in. Again he refused. "Trisha, there is a reason for you to swim back to the camp. And if you will trust me, I will show you what the reason is." I had once heard Jack say that people are the source of pain, and in my dream Jack was a huge source of my pain.

My mind was telling me a different message. The message was that I can't overcome my flesh man, so don't even try. *It is in the trying to overcome where the blessing is released, not just the overcoming.* This is a lesson I have just recently learned.

So I began my journey to swim back to camp. With each stroke of my arms I was thinking about how I was going to let Jack have it as soon as we returned to land. What was that? I had briefly noticed something struggling underneath the water. It was a small child entangled by a vine that was growing on the bottom of the lake. The vine had ensnared him and was choking the life out of him as he fought desperately to live. I dove down and, with my bare hands, I tore the vines from around him. I had only seconds to get him to the surface as I held his limp body under my arms and shot straight up as fast as my short little legs would kick. As soon as he hit air he took a deep gasp and the fluid in his lungs spewed all over me. I tucked him under my arm as I swam back to the shore with him. So this was what all the commotion was about. This child had gone missing. I could hear Jack's voice saying, "Now, do you understand why you had to swim to shore?"

Humbled by the fact that I was the one allowed to save this child, I suddenly realized that this was all about what is left of my life's purpose on this Earth. The boat represented a choice that I needed to make. I could choose the comfortableness of the boat (retirement), or I could choose to take a chance and discover a destiny with new challenges to help others save their lives.

Had I not been willing to take a risk and trust Jack's wisdom, to take a chance and use what ability I did have, no matter how insufficient I thought it was, the child would have died in the entanglements of that vine that ensnared him and caused him to become invisible in a place where no one could see him.

That is where my focus is today. I have to move forward with Him and His glory and His plan, and that can only be revealed through time with Him. Sometimes it can be a lonely place because, for me, during seasons of growth and transition, Father seems to place me in situations where it is only Him and I. Out of that I can bring those around me to speak into my life. Keep applying what Father is doing into your life and change comes.

When you focus on all things that have no Kingdom value, then you can become out of focus with purpose and destiny.

When all hell breaks loose, remember to focus on all Heaven breaking forth.

QUESTIONS TO PONDER

1. Can you define what it is, that as you do it and live it, you feel the Father's pleasure?

2. Another way to put this is, if money were not an issue, what would you do with your life? (In answering this question, you might discover more about your purpose.)

SAMPLE PRAYER

Father, forgive me for focusing more on the pain of my life than on the call of life. I give You permission to search me and see if there is any hurtful thing that would prevent me from receiving Your love and giving it away to my family and then to the world (see Ps. 139:23-24). *I make a choice this day to receive Your love. I choose to trust You with Your plan for me. I ask*

You to help me to dig deep into my soul and to know the things that the Holy Spirit has placed within me. I make a choice to discover those things and use them for Your Kingdom's sake. In Jesus' name.

Endnotes

1. Bill Johnson, "The Responsibility of Blessing," Bethel Church, Redding, CA, April 10, 2011.

2. Jack Hayford, *New Spirit-Filled Life Bible,* (Nashville: Thomas Nelson, Inc, 2002), 1226.

Final Thoughts

One of the things said about me after I made a choice to strengthen myself in the Lord and to live was, "Trisha, you are like a mother elephant." Just what every girl wants to hear! What I later discovered was that a mother elephant will stomp the ground until she can find water to give to her thirsty calves.

I love the meaning of names. It is the trendy thing today to name a child so that they follow the meaning of their name. I don't think that my mother had a clue what I would become when she named me. My name Patricia means "noble," and my nickname Trisha means "thirsty." I am thirsty and I will stomp the ground on behalf of all the calves that Father sends for me to give water to.

I find many times that people live entirely opposite of their names. So I want to encourage you to ask Him how to live out of who you are destined to become and not the pain of your past.

I want to leave you, the reader, with the challenge to become more than you can imagine you can ever be. I want to promise you that He really is sufficient in your life to bring you to its completion, having lived a full life with the words spoken over you, "You finished well."

I bless you to uncover the old habit patterns of thinking that have become strongholds in your life and that alienate you from intimacy first with Him, and then with those you love. Discover what that is so you will live a life *unbound* from life's entanglements.

Trisha Frost
I've loved you with an everlasting love (see Jer. 31:3)!

THE POWER TO CHOOSE

God gave each of us a precious gift that not even angels possess. He gave us the power of choice! We must use this power wisely.

Choose Life	Rather than Death
Choose to Love	Rather than to Hate
Choose to Forgive	Rather than Unforgiveness
Choose to Heal	Rather than to Wound
Choose to Give	Rather than to Take
Choose to Create Life	Rather than Destroy It
Choose to Embrace the Cross	Rather than to Walk in the Flesh
Choose to Change	Rather than to Remain the Way You Are

Change

Change: The greatest accomplishment now known to man
Yet, few of them attain it within their life span
For few men desire to be what they are not
They are afraid of what it might take to let go of their lot
To forfeit or give up or surrender their flesh for a cause
Is not at all masculine, but a part of the feminine laws
Laws that have led us to believe in such lies
That man cannot be tender or gentle, or have a soul tie
With only one woman to give his all to
To love her, to cherish her and to her only be true
To be kind to his family and live from his heart
A heart that heals hurts and repents for his part
Of wounding that gift that was given from Father above
A gift of His children to nurture and love
Yet Jack you seem to desire what our Father knows best
You have surrendered your flesh and put God to a test
A test to see if He could possibly change you
A change that would cause you to believe His love is true

That His plan for your life and your family
Would create an example for the entire world to see
To see a man who has let change have its place
Because change took you Jack, into the Father's Embrace
An embrace that we all experience now
Because your change has with it a commitment
of an eternal vow
That you will always walk in His purpose and Plan
And this will lead you to change again and again

Trisha Frost, October, 2002

About Jack and Trisha Frost

Jack and Trisha experienced many things through the 35 years of their relationship; some joyful and exciting, others disappointing and wounding. They lived, loved, and fought their way into finally finding their destiny. From their life's journey to find the love they had so desperately been seeking came a revelation of unconditional *agape* love that brought healing to their family and also to the lives of many families around the world as Jack traveled and shared their story. Now the message of *agape* continues in the life of Trisha and their children.

Jack had for years encouraged Trisha to tell her side of the story, saying to the Shiloh Place staff that "there is a Niagara Falls of teaching in her, waiting to be released." But until now the circumstances of life and ministry have kept her travel schedule at a minimum. Today is the hour of her release as one of many Shiloh Place teachers as we chart our way through new challenges of life without Jack. Trisha's life used to flow from feeling like an orphan, abandoned by her own loving father, and then by her husband; she felt she constantly had to take a back seat to Jack's other loves. Now she can take you on the journey to find your place in the heart of God as she shares the breakthrough of her own revelation of love at the culmination of her pathway to healing, foremost as a favored child of God, then also as a wife and a mother.

Trisha is ordained with The River Fellowship. She is a motivational speaker and if you would like to invite her to your event, you can contact her at Shiloh Place Ministries through the web or by phone 843-365-8990.

PO BOX 5798
North Myrtle Beach, SC 29597